The Jazz Rhythm Section

The Jazz Rhythm Section

A Manual for Band Directors

FUMI TOMITA

Published in cooperation with the
National Association for Music Education

ROWMAN & LITTLEFIELD
Lanham • Boulder • New York • London

Published in cooperation with the National Association for Music Education, 1806
Robert Fulton Drive, Reston, Virginia 20191; nafme.org

Published by Rowman & Littlefield
An imprint of The Rowman & Littlefield Publishing Group, Inc.
4501 Forbes Boulevard, Suite 200, Lanham, Maryland 20706
www.rowman.com

6 Tinworth Street, London SE11 5AL, United Kingdom

British Library Cataloguing in Publication Information Available

Library of Congress Cataloging-in-Publication Data
Names: Tomita, Fumi, 1971– author. | National Association for Music Education.
Title: The jazz rhythm section : a manual for band directors / Fumi Tomita.
Description: Lanham : Rowman & Littlefield, [2019] | "Published in
   cooperation with the National Association for Music Education."
Identifiers: LCCN 2018045847 (print) | LCCN 2018046569 (ebook) | ISBN
   9781475846874 (electronic) | ISBN 9781475846850 (cloth : alk. paper) |
   ISBN 9781475846867 (pbk. : alk. paper)
Subjects: LCSH: Big bands—Instruction and study. | Jazz—Instruction and
   study.
Classification: LCC MT733.7 (ebook) | LCC MT733.7 .T66 2019 (print) | DDC
   784.4/165—dc23
LC record available at https://lccn.loc.gov/2018045847

∞™ The paper used in this publication meets the minimum requirements of
American National Standard for Information Sciences—Permanence of Paper
for Printed Library Materials, ANSI/NISO Z39.48-1992.

Printed in the United States of America

Contents

Foreword

Shigefumi (Fumi) Tomita has managed to put together a very enlightening and impressive book for teachers and students at all levels of skill.

Wow, *The Jazz Rhythm Section* is a fantastic contribution to the jazz education arena!

I have known Fumi and had the pleasure of working with him for more than three years in various educational and professional capacities. During those years, he has proven to be a very creative and insightful educator/performer who carries out his tasks as a true professional and a talented musician. He has a wonderful work ethic and commitment to the field of jazz education, which has been demonstrated in his high level of string bass performance and teaching skills in the classroom. I am thrilled to have the opportunity to share my insight regarding this book, as well as my personal relationship with this talented bassist and educator. I feel that he has truly assembled materials in this book that will fit the needs of educators at all levels who are interested in helping rhythm section players reach their full potential.

After reviewing each chapter in this important volume, I believe this book will become the resource of choice for teachers and students who are serious about teaching and learning how to function comfortably in the rhythm section. I am certain that assembling this very thoughtful work was a long and complex, yet fun, effort by Fumi. This work establishes a fresh approach to educating the novice player about his or her role on the piano, bass, drum set, or guitar in a combo and jazz ensemble setting. The examples are presented step by step in a clear and accessible fashion for each instrument throughout this book.

Various styles, including swing, Latin, Afro-Cuban, rock, and so on, are introduced in a well-defined manner. Also included are proper ways to set up the rhythm section, solid rehearsal techniques, a list of equipment options . . . you name it—it's provided!

The Jazz Rhythm Section is bound to become the handy resource of choice not only for students but also for teachers and professionals. Its fresh approach, clear examples, and easy accessibility for a variety of styles make it a versatile volume to have in your library. I salute Fumi for bringing this book to life, and I highly recommend it. Enjoy!

Dr. Willie L. Hill Jr.
Director, Fine Arts Center
Professor, Music Education
University of Massachusetts Amherst

Introduction

The rhythm section is the foundation of any jazz group, whether big band or combo. I view the rhythm section as the red carpet on which the rest of the band can strut their stuff: the nicer it is, the easier it will be for the band to play. The rhythm section provides the groove that serves as the glue binding the entire band together. Since its role is so critical in the success of any jazz group, it is important that all jazz directors have a basic understanding of how each instrument works in order for the players in the rhythm section to groove together.

This book is intended for jazz directors with little to no jazz experience. However, even those with knowledge or experience in jazz can benefit from this book, as they are often faced with the same problems relating to equipment and performance practice: How do you get the bass player or drummer to swing? How does a pianist or guitarist comp? Rehearsing saxes and brass is, in a way, not so different from rehearsing different sections of an orchestra or marching band. But the rhythm section players have a different function that is specific to jazz.

While I outline the basic performance practices of each instrument, I also discuss each instrument's unique equipment and setup issues. Critical to playing jazz well is using the proper equipment to obtain the ideal sound. Since there is a lot of crossover with other styles of music, it is important to understand that jazz players have different equipment needs than rock players.

Acoustic and electric bass is an obvious example, but not so obvious is the need for an archtop guitar sound when the guitarist has a solid-body guitar. Cymbals and drums for rock bands are very different from the ones used in jazz groups. Not only is the construction different, but the drum-tuning philosophy is also completely different. Still, it is often impossible to change the equipment you have to deal with, so I also go over options on how to improve what you have to achieve the sound that you need.

The information contained in this book was learned and gathered over years of performance and self-instruction. I am a professional jazz bassist (primarily acoustic), but I initially learned piano, drums, and guitar as a teenager. I never stopped playing those instruments, and over the years I have continued to grow on them (primarily piano and guitar) through my own self-study of jazz improvisation, composition, and arranging.

For additional insights, I interviewed a number of bassists, drummers, pianists, and guitarists. I also researched numerous instructional videos and websites on the internet. Particularly helpful were the forum discussions from various gear websites, where I learned that the various "best gut string"–style debates on bass websites were easily applicable to other instruments. In the opening stages of this book, I realized that not many people would search out this information on their own. It is an almost overwhelming task to learn about four different instruments and how they function together. This book is a starting point and a reference for understanding the basic equipment and performance practice for each instrument to help them work together and to create a solid groove.

Numerous people have helped me during the writing of this book. I would like to single out a few who were particularly helpful: Carl Clements, Bob Sabin, Russ Spiegel, Jesse Simon, Mark Micklethwaite, Lou Rainone, and Doug Abrahms; Forest Loomis-Dulong, Ben Powell, and Niall McCarthy; Gernot Bernroider, Bob Weiner, Bob Ferrier, and Cathy Jensen-Hole (for the use of their equipment); and Eric Berlin (for photography). Special thanks go to Dave Rivello for his last-minute help; to my colleague and mentor Felipe Salles for encouraging me to publish this book; and, finally, to my parents for their support.

My hope is that this book will be of some use to you the band director, as a starting point to better understanding the rhythm section, to augment your knowledge of jazz performance, and to enhance the sound of your band.

1

Rhythm Section Basics

In jazz there is a saying that every member of the band is a drummer. This is because everyone in the band needs to be playing good time and to be feeling the same groove. Time, rhythm, and groove are so important that there is a section created to emphasize them, the rhythm section, and they are the foundation of the jazz ensemble.

A unique aspect of the rhythm section in jazz is that they are often playing and improvising throughout *the entire performance*. Unless otherwise notated to solo, saxophones and brass do not improvise at all and stick to the written page. Rhythm section parts, however, are often nothing more than a chord chart with rhythmic slashes or a series of repeated figures. The implication is that they are asked to "fill in the blanks" and improvise their part. Therefore, rhythm section players need to have a basic knowledge of jazz performance practice particular to their instrument.

Another unique aspect of the rhythm section is the lack of a natural hierarchical system. Everyone in the rhythm section works independently together in forging a solid groove, and no single instrument is the obvious section leader. If there is an unofficial leader, this role is often determined by skill level, personality, or age, depending on the situation. As a result, there exist many critical relationships and interrelationships within the rhythm section, and at the core there are two interconnecting layers: the bass and drums providing the groove and the chord players (guitar and piano) outlining the harmonies.

BASS AND DRUMS

The heart of the rhythm section is the bass and drums. Together they set the tone of the song by establishing the basic pulse and time feel or groove. As a team, they are so important that for some people the bass and drums are the rhythm section.

No matter what the feel of the song is, be it swing, bossa nova, or funk, the bass and drums provide the basic groove and foundation of the song. If they are not in sync, they disrupt everything that happens above them. Therefore, they have to be listening to each other, and their parts need to "lock in" together before elaborating on their parts with fills and so forth. Since they work together, it should come as no surprise that their parts complement each other perfectly. The following is a style guide to better understand how their parts are connected.

Swing

Swing feel is governed by swing eighth notes, and this is perhaps the most difficult concept for beginners to grasp. Learning how to "swing," students are commonly told to think of swing eighths as being the first and third triplets of an eighth-note triplet. But in practice, swing eighth notes fall somewhere between the even eighth note, which falls halfway through the beat and the third eighth note of an eighth-note triplet (see figure 1.1).

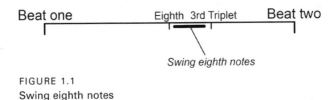

FIGURE 1.1
Swing eighth notes

The problem is there is no exact placement of the second eighth note, and it is often determined by tempo. At slower tempos (quarter note = around 90 or below), the second swing eighth note falls closer to the triplet, and at fast tempos (quarter note = 180 and above), that note falls closer to the even eighth. If one maintains the triplet feel at faster tempos, then the music sounds square, compounded by the fact that downbeats are often played short (see figure 1.2).

FIGURE 1.2

This is remedied by having students play longer downbeats and putting a slight emphasis on the second eighth note rather than exaggerating it (see figure 1.3).

FIGURE 1.3

With bass and drums, the quarter notes obviously need to be in sync, but it is more important for the groove that the eighth notes line up. For the drummer, this means listening to the bassist's quarter notes. Watching the bassist's right-hand fingers provides a visual representation of the beat and enables drummers to see when the strings are being plucked. Since drummers often vary their ride cymbal pattern, bassists should not watch the drummer's hand. Instead, they should be listening to the ride cymbal pattern for the drummer's time feel and match it with their own.

At slow to medium swing tempos, they should be feeling/tapping out quarter notes with an emphasis on beats 2 and 4. This is accentuated with the hi-hat that closes on those beats, and so the bassist should be aware of this as well as listening for the ride cymbal.

Together, the low bass notes mesh well with the high-pitched ride cymbal. Listen to the smooth blend between drummer Jimmy Cobb and bassist Paul Chambers on Miles Davis's "So What" from the album *Kind of Blue*. The shimmer of Cobb's ride cymbal matches perfectly with Chambers's bass notes. Their pulse is equally in sync. Next time you listen to a jazz recording, notice the blend of the bass and drums in sound, timbre, and time feel.

Shuffle

The shuffle feel is based on a swing feel with a stronger triplet feel and is typically played at a medium tempo. Yet it differs from swing feel in that the rhythm section parts tend to rely on repetitive patterns. For inexperienced students, learning shuffles is a good precursor to swing feel. Plus, the repetitive parts make it easier for the bass and drums (and the rhythm section altogether) to jell together as their parts are simpler with a focus on rhythm.

Fast Swing

Fast tempos present a different challenge as drummers and especially bassists often lack the stamina to make it through an entire chart. The best plan for them (and everyone in the band) is to play with a lighter touch and to not play with so much force and energy. It will sound softer, but this will help them relax at the faster tempo in addition to conserving energy and reducing the frantic feel.

Also, tapping quarter notes at quarter note = 160+ is no easy task! You'll tire everyone out in no time, so fast tempos are also best felt in a "two" feel. The bass and drum parts don't change; instead they just tap and/or feel beats 1 and 3. If the tempo is very fast, then it might be better to feel the beat as a "one" feel where only beat 1 is tapped out. This might seem counterintuitive in music that emphasizes beats 2 and 4, but to maintain the tempo and the feel, it is simpler and more accurate to tap your foot and/or feel the beat at a slower pace. It also lines up with the swing eighth notes, which tend to become straighter as the tempo increases.

Jazz Ballad

Jazz ballads are difficult for everyone due to the slow tempo and exposed parts. Swing eighths are still the undercurrent, and the bass and drums usually play in a "two" feel. A good way to maintain slow tempos is to feel and say the triplet subdivision of the beat. At fast tempos, swing eighth notes become straighter, but at slower tempos (quarter note = 90 and below), they start sounding like triplets. Therefore, subdividing triplets while maintaining time emphasizes this time feel and promotes forward motion.

Bassists can also walk through the chord changes to generate more energy. Another popular tactic is to change to a double-time feel for the solos to help accelerate the energy of the performance—double-time meaning that the pace of the chords is the same but the band plays twice as fast where there are two bars of the double-time feel in the space of one bar (see figure 1.4).

A good example can be heard on Miles Davis's version of "'Round Midnight" from the album 'Round About Midnight, where the theme is played in ballad tempo and the solos are in double time.

FIGURE 1.4
Double time

Changing to medium swing is not a bad thing, but it avoids the problem of feeling comfortable at a slow tempo. Plus, when this occurs, it often feels like a different song. Students need to learn how to generate energy at a slow tempo. As jazz band director, you can help by counting off ballads that aren't too slow, starting at quarter note = 80.

Working on slow tempos is difficult but, interestingly, make fast tempos easier, since fast tempos tend to be felt as either a "two feel" or a "one feel." Since they complement each other in this way, it is a good idea to work on both tempos in rehearsal.

Latin Jazz

Under the large heading of "Latin jazz," there are many substyles that jazz big bands play. We'll look at bossa nova, samba, and Afro-Cuban, as these are the most common styles played and the easiest to play. Regardless of style, they are all governed by a straight eighth-note pulse rather than swing eighth notes.

Most Latin jazz styles feature large percussion sections, which, in jazz, are typically reduced to a single drum set part. As a result, drum set parts are quite polyrhythmic and take time to master. Bass parts, by contrast, are simpler. They typically emphasize the root and the fifth while maintaining a rhythmic ostinato, rendering the bass as more of a percussion instrument.

Bossa nova/Samba

The most important element of the Brazilian bossa nova is that it is in cut time, or "two" feel, even though it is written in 4/4 time. Originally composed in 2/4, there is a slight accent on beats 1 and 3, accentuated by the bass and the bass drum. Having the bassists feel 2/2 will help emphasize the subtle poly-rhythmic aspects of bossa nova. Meanwhile, the drum part maintains the 4/4 part with an eighth-note pulse on the ride or hi-hat and the rimshots, while lining up with the bass in the bass drum (see figure 1.5).

FIGURE 1.5
Bass and drum parts in bossa nova

Remember that bossa nova is not rock! It's about subtlety and sensitivity in the rhythm section while emphasizing the half-time feel, so bass and drums should strive for a gentler pulse. Bassists can even reduce their parts to just half notes to emphasize the ballad-like feel. The Brazilian samba has all the aspects of bossa nova except at a faster tempo.

For good examples of bossa nova and samba, I recommend the famous Stan Getz recordings with Joao Gilberto and the *Big Band Bossa Nova* album with Gary McFarland. A good blend of jazz and authentic Brazilian rhythms can be heard on these recordings and is a good place to start.

Afro-Cuban

Afro-Cuban music is equally as polyrhythmic and emphasizes three-against-two. Written in 6/8, the dotted quarter note is emphasized, making it feel like it is the quarter note with the quarter note feeling like quarter-note triplets. Once this fact is pointed out then the music becomes easier to feel and understand (see figures 1.6 and 1.7).

The drum part in Afro-Cuban music plays both pulses and can be quite confusing. However, the dotted quarter note pulse is in the closed hi-hat, and this is what the bassist should be listening for (see figure 1.8).

FIGURE 1.6
3:2

FIGURE 1.7
2:3

FIGURE 1.8
Common Afro-Cuban drum part

Rock

Like Latin jazz, rock is often based on a straight eighth-note pulse. Like shuffles, they also tend to be based on repetitive patterns, making them easier to understand and play. How the bass and drums fit together in these styles will vary depending upon the song, the tempo, and more. Generally speaking, the basic eighth-note pulse is played by the drums on the hi-hat or the ride cymbal. Just as in swing feel, both the bassist and the drummer should be listening for each other's eighth-note feel to determine the pulse and achieve a common ground on the time feel.

Funk

Funk differs from rock with the emphasis on syncopation that often includes sixteenth notes. Depending on the level of your band, this could be a good way to learn those more complex rhythms. Figure 1.9 shows a typical funk bassline and drum part.

FIGURE 1.9
Common bass and drum parts in funk

Notice how the fourth sixteenth note of the first beat is played by both the bass and the snare drum. A solid rhythm section will have that particular note played in sync by the bassist and drummer. As there are many variations of rock, soul, and funk grooves, bassists and drummers should be familiar with the other's part to understand how they fit together.

Groove

In the end, the bass and drums establish the groove of the song. This is achieved by having good time (neither slowing down nor speeding up), by matching each other's time feels, and by playing at an appropriate volume level where both instruments are equally prominent. From Miles Davis to Led Zeppelin to Snarky Puppy, all grooving rhythm sections contain these traits.

Good time is achieved from listening and by consistent metronome practice. While everything should be practiced with a metronome, it is particularly helpful to place the metronome on different beats to improve one's time feel. For example, instead of having the metronome sound quarter notes, have it sound on beats 2 and 4. For example, if the tempo is quarter note = 120, then place the metronome at 60. (See the subsection titled "Metronome Exercises" on page 18 for more information.)

Matching time feels is best done by listening and feeling the other's pulse. No matter the style, the subdivisions of the quarter note (either the eighth or the sixteenth note) dictate the groove. For example, Stevie Wonder's "Superstition" features a solid groove at a fairly slow tempo. However, one needs to be aware of the swing sixteenth-note undercurrent that guides the song, creating a subtle double-time feel that greatly influences the flow of the quarter notes. Although the bass part does not include sixteenth notes, if they are not felt that way, then his or her quarter notes will sound wrong and out of sync with the drums. Groove is an imprecise art, so drummers and bassists need to be particularly aware of how the other is feeling the subdivisions.

For example, if the bass player feels a rock chart with a slight accent on the off beat, but the drummer feels it with an accent on the downbeat, then there is a serious contradiction of opinion, which will result in no groove. This needs to be evened out, and one or the other needs to adjust or they need to meet halfway. If the music does not feel right to you, start with the bass and drums to see whether they are together.

Finally, everyone must be playing at an even volume so that the groove can be felt. If all you hear is bass, then there is no groove. When listening to recordings, pay attention to the bass and drums to understand how they sync together. You will see that groove can be many things, from intense to laid back. Groove is very much the interaction between the instrumentalists.

A good way to learn about groove is to listen to a recording of the song you are playing and hear how the bass and drums are lining up together. This is a good idea to do anyway with the whole band. But if you or the players are unfamiliar with the grooves of your charts, then it is a necessary prerequisite to playing your chart well. Even during rehearsals, spending time listening to recordings of professionals playing the music is educational for everyone.

COMPING INSTRUMENTS

Working with the bass and drums is the chordal player providing the harmonies, typically piano or guitar (or both). Though vibraphone can also fit into this role, this section will focus primarily on the more commonly used piano and guitar.

Working with Bass and Drums

For comping instruments, unless it is their turn to solo, their job is strictly support. However, like the bass they also have a strong rhythmic function and work together with the bass and drums to help provide the groove of the song. Since they aren't playing the whole time, they need to be listening to the bass and drums for the pulse and to feel and figure out where their rhythms "fit." Harmonically, pianists and guitarists should aim to use rootless voicings and rely on the bassists' roots to ground the chord. Doing so also creates unique sonic roles between the bass and the comping instruments.

In the case where the pianist is stronger than the bassist and drummer, that pianist should lead the rhythm section by playing strong time. Emphasizing downbeats will help the bass and drums along.

Comping Instruments and Bass

At the beginning level, these players learn how to identify each other's parts and to make sure that they are in sync with each other. This will also help them ensure that they are in the same place and is a good way for them to not feel so isolated in their role, particularly if one is stronger than the other. After all, they are providing the same harmonic foundation, so there is a lot of overlap. For example, many jazz charts have the piano player's left hand doubling the bass part. While this is done for textural reasons, upright and fretless bassists can work on their intonation in this way.

Comping Instruments and Drums

While the comping instruments are providing rhythmic punctuations with their voicings, they should also be made aware that the drummer is also contributing rhythmic punctuations on the snare drum and/or bass drum. Pianist Red Garland and drummer "Philly" Joe Jones in Miles Davis's first great quintet blended their comping so well that the piano chords and snare drum sounded like they were played by the same person. Since the piano was often playing on the "ands" of beats 2 and 4, it was easy for the drums to catch those on the snare.

Sometimes this rhythm section (with bassist Paul Chambers) would play planned backgrounds during solos. These figures were derived from the swing era, when various horn players would introduce background figures that the rest of the band would pick up on. A good example of their interaction can be heard on "Blues by Five" from the album *Cookin'* by Miles Davis. Behind John Coltrane's tenor saxophone solo at 3:31, they play a repeated four-bar figure. You can hear from 2:59 how they imply it without actually playing it.

It does not need to be this obvious, but such backgrounds are a good way for the rhythm section to learn to integrate as a unit. Especially in a combo situation, introducing these figures to your rhythm section players teaches them a vocabulary of comping from which they can learn to play together.

Multiple Instruments Comping Together

At the introductory level, guitarists and pianists need to learn voicings, so often it is best to have them actively involved. However, too many comping instruments can create a cluttered sound. One way to maintain a tidy sound is to have one instrument play punctuation-type rhythms in the middle register while the other plays pads or held chords in the upper register. This helps define their own roles and sonic territory while preventing them from getting in each other's way.

At the intermediate to advanced levels, there should only be one comping instrument per soloist. This means that comping instruments have to get used to following who they are comping for. However, it also allows for more freedom for the soloist and the comping player and invites a closer conversation between the two.

RHYTHM SECTION AND THE BAND

Once the bass, drums, and the comping instrument players are grooving along, the next step is to make sure that they are playing in an uncluttered manner that does not detract from the soloist, the ensemble, or whatever else is going on above them. There are a couple of different things that rhythm section members should be aware of when playing.

Developing Peripheral Hearing

Just as there is peripheral vision, there is also peripheral hearing that all musicians (not just jazz rhythm section players) must learn to use. Rhythm section players should be primarily focused on their part while simultaneously keeping their other rhythm section mates in their rearview mirrors. But they also shouldn't forget the soloist who is right in front of them! This is a skill that takes time to learn, but alerting students to this fact will help them become better accompanists.

Volume

One way for a good rhythm section to blend together is to make sure that all musicians are playing at the same volume. This means adjusting their touch and the volumes on their amplifiers. Over- or underwhelming volume or attack affects the perception of the performance and can throw off the momentum of a band, so rhythm section players need to be aware of this.

Less Is More

Beginning musicians tend to overplay: drummers and bassists may play too many fills or guitarists and pianists may overcomp. A rowdy rhythm section can easily overpower the band. It is important to remind them that they are playing as a team and that their basic part is a strong enough contribution to the band. It takes a certain amount of restraint to do the minimum, but "less is more" certainly applies here. The goal is to have a clean rhythm section sound that either the soloist or the ensemble can easily rest upon.

Rhythm Section and the Soloist

While the above material certainly applies when there is a soloist, the role widens and they can be more actively involved by interacting with the soloist. How they do so will largely depend upon the individual player or the moment, but by asserting a stronger presence, they can complement the direction of the solo.

Pianist Wynton Kelly's comping behind Miles Davis on "Pfrancing," from the album *Someday My Prince Will Come*, at 1:18 to 3:02 is a good example of such active comping. In the beginning of Davis's solo, Kelly does not comp (known as *strolling*) for the first two choruses save for a few choice notes. When he does come in, his rich voicings and appropriate comping rhythms manage to engage Davis without overpowering him. Another good example is pianist Herbie Hancock's comping behind tenor saxophonist George Coleman on "All of You," from Miles Davis's album *My Funny Valentine*, at 4:53 to 8:11. This live recording depicts a band that is used to playing with each other night after night; as a result, Hancock follows Coleman's reharmonizations and seems to know exactly when to leave space and when to play, even engaging in call and response with Coleman at 7:38 to 7:58.

LAYOUT

Equally important to the success of a good rhythm section is how they are positioned relative to each other. Rhythm section members need to be properly located for visual contact and optimal listening habits. Since the rhythm section and the whole band rests on the bassist and drummer, they should be right next to each other, with the bassist on the ride cymbal side of the drums. Sometimes beginning bassists are placed on the hi-hat side of the drums, and this enables them to "lock in" their part with the hi-hat. However, since the ride cymbal is the heart of jazz drumming, it is better for the bassist to listen to that instead and to be on the ride cymbal side of the drum set; the hi-hat will still be audible.

Since the bassist does double duty providing rhythmic and harmonic support, they should be between the drums and piano. This location enables them to lock in with either instrument and reminds them of their dual role. Therefore, the piano is always on the bassist's right side. The bass amplifier should be placed in the back between the bass and the drums so that the sound travels toward the drummer as well.

Since the musicians do not really speak to each other during a performance, it is important for them to be able to see each other. For this reason, the drums and piano should position themselves at an angle. Setting up in this way will not only help each player be aware of the other's presence but also promote aural and visual communication between them (see figure 1.10).

The guitarist is usually seated in front between the bassist, who is in the back, and the pianist. This allows the guitarist to fully integrate into the

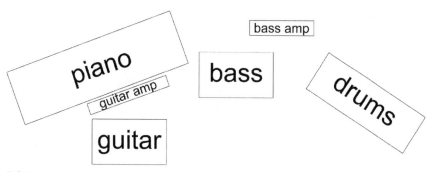

FIGURE 1.10
Rhythm section layout

rhythm section when he or she is comping. Plus, by being next to the pianist, they can talk to each other and easily communicate who is comping
for whom. The guitar amplifier is typically behind the guitarist and usually
under the grand piano.

In general, whoever is playing with amplification should not stand directly
in front of the amplifier. Bass players will be blocking the sound, rendering
them quieter than they actually are. Guitar players won't hear themselves very
well since the higher frequencies travel straight out, bypassing the guitarists'
ears. Thus, they need to make sure the amp is pointing toward their ears by
positioning the amp as far back as possible. Another option is to place it on
a chair or at an angle, especially if the amplifier is small or is of low wattage.
Finally, avoid having amplifiers next to each other, as there is often some
overlap in frequencies, resulting in ambiguous sonic territory. For example,
if the bass and guitar amps are right next to each other and the guitarist plays
in the low register, he or she will be disturbing the bassist's sonic range. A
singular sonic space for each instrument is critical toward a good-sounding
rhythm section.

REHEARSAL TECHNIQUES

Rhythm section rehearsing can begin with just the bass and drums, then
adding the comping instruments. This way you are building your foundation from the ground up, and the more solid this is, the better the band will
be. It will help you to understand how the parts function together if you are
unfamiliar with them.

Establishing the Groove with Count Offs

Since the rhythm section provides the time feel for the band, it's important for you as the jazz band director to inspire this groove. One way to do so is to sing the subdivisions of the song while counting off the tune, or even during the tune. This is one of the most important factors for the success of a chart. Too many times jazz directors (and bandleaders on gigs) count off tunes by only snapping their fingers on beats 2 and 4 without any indication as to what the basic pulse is. This is confusing, and it requires musicians to take time to figure out what the quarter note is. This is not a good way to start. No matter the style, the basic pulse needs to be seen, heard, and felt.

On top of demonstrating the tempo, it is helpful to sing the underlying groove that propels the song. Most often it is eighth notes, but some funk tunes have a sixteenth-note subdivision while some bluesy ballads might have a triplet subdivision. Whether swing, bossa nova, or rock, this will help generate a stronger groove. Simply scat eighth notes or sing a bit of the melody of the tune while counting off. It may feel silly singing nonsense syllables that often sound absurd, but this is the secret to understanding groove.

Beginning musicians have a difficult time maintaining and hearing tempo, so it is important to use the count off as a focal point for students. Take your time snapping your fingers or singing the melody as you are setting the tone for the performance that is to follow.

Swing

Different feels call for methods of counting off charts. For jazz swing tunes, unless the tune is a ballad or up tempo, pretend you are the drummer playing quarter notes on the ride cymbal. With your arm sticking out, pretend that you are playing an invisible ride cymbal by lightly bouncing quarter notes with your wrist. Begin snapping your fingers with the same hand on beats 2 and 4 (see figure 1.11).

'play' quarter notes on the imaginary ride cymbal

snap fingers on 'two' and 'four'

FIGURE 1.11
Count off method for swing

This may take some practice, but now everyone can *see* where your pulse is and better establish the groove and tempo. Next, start scatting the melody to the chart you are playing. To get a nice flow going, vary your syllables and try not to repeat the same syllable twice in a row.

Bossa nova

For bossa nova, one can set the pulse by "wiping" eighth notes with both hands (the motion with your hands when you're finished with something) while tapping or stomping half notes (see figure 1.12).

FIGURE 1.12
Establishing the time feel in bossa nova

If the tempo is slow enough, you can rub your palms together (imitating a shaker-like sound) in an eighth-note feel for a smoother sound. Either way, you should sing a little bit of the melody to set the tone. Bossas are also commonly counted off with the preceding eighth note to emphasize the straight eighth-note pulse (see figure 1.13).

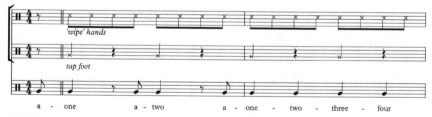

FIGURE 1.13
Count off method for bossa nova

Rock

For rock (as well as soul or funk), I recommend tapping or snapping or stomping out the quarter note while clapping beats 2 and 4. In essence, no matter the style you should communicate the basic underlying pulse of the song being played, as this is where the groove begins.

Of course, the tone of your voice can greatly influence the groove and the way the band plays. For example, you should probably count off a soft ballad differently from how you would count off a bright rock chart. Similarly, your hand or body motions should reflect the mood of the chart. Your energy during the count off can sometimes make all the difference. If you find the rhythm section dragging the tempo, then go in front of them and sing the subdivisions to them while they are playing.

Metronome Exercises

The key to a good rhythm section is having everybody play with good time. Actually, this is also the key to a good-sounding band: when *everyone* has good time. Remember, the essence of the jazz ensemble is that every member of the band (including the director) is a drummer. Everybody is responsible for the time, and this can't be emphasized enough. Rhythm section players are the most responsible for outlining the time and have a stronger rhythmic role. After all, they are the *rhythm* section.

A good way to emphasize this fact is to rehearse with a metronome. At the end of the day, the whole band should be aware of the time. If your rhythm section is having problems maintaining the tempo, then have them practice playing along with a metronome in rehearsal. This will alert them to the importance of keeping time.

With an electric metronome (on your smartphone or otherwise), simply plug it into an amplifier (with an ⅛-inch to ¼-inch adapter) and turn it up loud enough for everyone to hear while playing. It is an excellent exercise in playing good time and helps internalize the tempo while, most important, promoting metronome practice on their own time.

For jazz swing tunes at a nice medium tempo, the metronome should be placed on beats 2 and 4. Because of the importance of feeling the music on these beats, it helps to also practice this way. For example, if the tune is at quarter note = 120, then place the metronome at 60 and count it off. At first it may be difficult to feel, but it soon becomes easier. Think of it as just hearing the snare drum on a pop song.

If it is too difficult to play the actual chart, have the students play or sing something they are familiar with; it can be something as simple as singing the roots of a blues chord progression. Vocalizing time is a great way to internalize time.

At ballad tempos, the metronome should be felt as quarter notes. Regardless of feel (rock, swing, bossa nova), students should practice with the metronome in this way to develop a stronger time feel.

FINAL THOUGHTS

As important as it is to conceive of the rhythm section as one unit, it is also
important to understand each instrument's unique equipment, setup, and
performance practice issues. The following chapters detail the main instruments of the rhythm section: bass, drums, piano, and guitar.

Bass

By outlining both the rhythm and the harmony, the bass holds a powerful position in the rhythm section. It is also the only one in the group, except sometimes for the baritone saxophone or the bass trombone, playing in that low register. Hearing that fundamental root note is essential, as jazz charts tend to feature harmonies that are often thick and dissonant with sevenths, ninths, altered tones, and more. In big band ensembles, saxophones and brass can adjust their intonation to the bass since it is the only instrument that maintains the lowest end of the frequency range. Having the pianist play left-hand bass lines on a keyboard is better than no bass at all.

ROLE

Within a section that works together to provide a foundation, the bass is the foundational instrument within the rhythm section. Bassists do double duty in establishing the groove with the drums while simultaneously laying out the harmonic structure with the piano and/or guitar, making them the anchor of the rhythm section. The domino effect is evident, as having a strong bassist results in a stronger rhythm section, which results in a stronger big band.

EQUIPMENT

For jazz band, either acoustic or electric bass is acceptable. Jazz groups started becoming active from the early 1900s, and although tuba was used in the beginning, acoustic bass has been the primary instrument of choice for swing-based jazz due to the percussive attack that pizzicato bass produces. As rock, soul, and funk charts became incorporated into jazz from the late 1960s, the electric bass also became an accepted instrument in jazz ensembles. In emergency scenarios, tuba or sousaphone will work as well, but keep in mind that your repertoire will then be limited to early New Orleans–style jazz, rock, funk, or any jazz-related style without walking bass lines.

Acoustic Bass

The sound of swing and, especially, big band, is often equated with acoustic instruments. So for jazz band, acoustic bass (or upright or double bass)

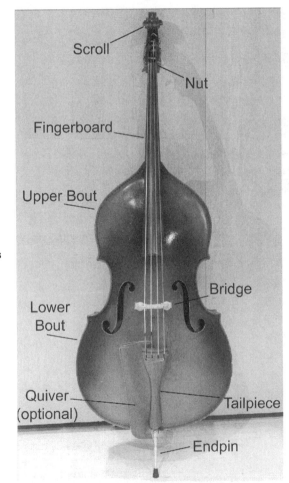

FIGURE 2.1
Acoustic bass

is the ideal instrument. For many people, the sound and look of the instrument equals jazz, and the biggest benefit of the acoustic bass is the sound. That round, woody tone spells out a strong, fundamental note with all of the overtones that is often equated with swing and cannot be replicated exactly on electric bass.

However, for young bassists the downsides of playing the instrument are often overwhelming. For starters, a lot of stamina is required just to *hold* the instrument as jazz bassists stand while playing and, like all members of the rhythm section, tend to play throughout the whole chart without a break. Acoustic bass strings are also very thick with high action (action meaning the distance between the strings and the fingerboard), and the constant finger contact results in blisters and sore shoulders and backs. Electric bassists used to a smaller neck and thinner strings are often intimidated by the larger acoustic bass. However, with proper setup, the acoustic bass can be a safe and fun instrument.

Setup

Setup refers to the small adjustments one can make to help ease the playability of the instrument. Due to physical issues in playing the instrument, proper setup can greatly aid the young bassist. More than any other instrument in the jazz ensemble, the acoustic bass can cause serious injury. Therefore, it is important to do what you can so that the student is not playing in any pain. One of the most important things to consider is making sure the bass is outfitted with bridge adjusters (see figure 2.2).

These metal wheels in the bridge rotate and allow one to adjust the action. Having high action on a bass results in a louder acoustic sound, and for

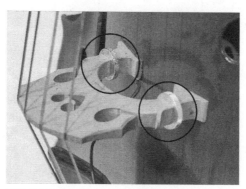

FIGURE 2.2
Bridge adjusters

classical bassists, this is a necessity since they play unamplified. However, it requires more energy to pluck the string and can wear out any bassist. Lowering the action makes the bass quieter in volume but much easier to pluck, and the benefits are worthwhile.

With a felt tip pen, mark a line on the top of both bridge adjusters. This will act as a reference point when you rotate the wheel. To lower the action, while holding on to the bridge for stability simply turn the wheel (usually to the right) until you see the black line again; to raise the action, simply turn the wheel in reverse.

Acoustic basses are finicky instruments, and as the seasons change, so does the bass: in the winter the wood tends to expand, creating lower action, while in the summer, the wood shrinks and the action becomes much higher. Bridge adjusters make life as a bassist (and band director) easier and will also prevent any further issues with the bass, as high action puts a lot of pressure on the neck and the body of the bass, resulting in annoying open seams and cracks. If you or your student are renting or buying a bass, make sure it has the adjusters installed.

Strings

Another important consideration with regard to setup and playability is the strings on the bass. Orchestral strings are designed for arco and thus lack the punch, sustain, and volume required for pizzicato playing. Assuming your bass will be used in orchestra and jazz band, you should have a versatile string ideal for both arco and pizz. Thomastik Spirocores or Weichs and Pirastro's Evah Pirazzi strings are reasonably priced and will last a long time.

Bass Humidifier

The last item that I recommend is a minibass humidifier called a Dampit. Consisting of a rubber tube holding a long, thin sponge, it can save your bass during the winter from cracks and open seams. Simply soak the tube in water, strain the excess water, and place the Dampit inside one of the "f" holes of the bass. Keep the bass in its case and change the water every few days, and your bass should remain in good condition. Overall, it is an affordable way to maintain the instrument.

Pickups and Preamplifier

Though acoustic bassists work on getting a strong acoustic tone, the volume is insufficient for a combo, let alone a big band. Therefore, the instrument needs to be amplified and requires a pickup. An acoustic bass pickup allows the instrument to be amplified and is generally not too difficult to install, though in an emergency situation you can use a microphone.

Getting a good sound from an amplifier is always a challenge with acoustic bass, and if you wish, you can purchase a separate preamplifier (preamp) to improve the sound. The preamp has an equalizer that can greatly enhance the sound of a bass, which can be particularly effective for cheap plywood basses and low-quality amplifiers. Both K&K Bass Max and Fishman produce solid preamps that allow you to equalize (EQ) the sound on the preamp. In order to use one, simply plug your quarter-inch cable from the bass to the preamp and then plug another quarter-inch cable between the preamp and the amplifier. Today the quality of electric basses is such that you should get a good enough sound without the use of a preamp.

Purchasing an Acoustic Bass

In purchasing an acoustic bass, you should expect to pay at least $1,500–$2,500 for a good plywood bass (with a soft case). If you buy anything below this price, it should be done in consultation with a professional bassist. Acoustic basses require maintenance, so you should invest in one with the least amount of issues. Cheap basses on eBay or ones sold through music education companies tend to be poorly constructed and more trouble than they're worth. The instrument has to be able to withstand changes in weather and students learning how not to bump it into doors, so purchasing a quality instrument is worthwhile. Used basses are generally preferred as the wood will have settled in, but newer companies like Shen and Upton are making excellent basses at affordable prices.

Electric Bass

Electric bass, by contrast, is low maintenance and easy to play. Being a smaller instrument with thinner strings, the electric bass is far friendlier to the young bassist. Electric basses are more sturdily constructed and are generally

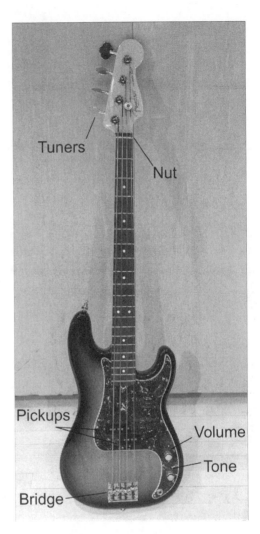

FIGURE 2.3
Electric bass—with one pickup

built to withstand changes in temperature, so setup is rarely an issue. A badly bowed neck can be repaired by turning the truss rod, but in general necks rarely move to the point of unplayability. Keep the instrument in its case and it should stay in good condition for a long time.

Types of Electric Basses

Electric basses come fretted or fretless, and either is fine to use. Fretted basses are most common, and they are much easier to play. Fretless basses require precise left-hand technique and are harder to play in tune. Jaco Pastorius popularized the instrument through his own solo work and recordings with Weather Report.

Electric basses are commonly four-stringed instruments, but some have extra strings with a low B or a high C (or even both). They include either passive or active electronics, where active pickups are typically powered by a nine-volt battery (usually installed through a panel in the back of the bass). Active basses provide a stronger signal (and tone) from the instrument itself. If you are a band director, this usually won't affect you, as most beginner basses use passive electronics. However, the one concern with active basses is that the nine-volt battery could run out at any minute. So, if your student has one, then, for safety, make sure you replace the battery prior to a concert.

Some students will already have an electric bass as starter kits (bass, patch cord, and small practice amplifier), so it really isn't necessary to purchase one. If you do need one, then, depending on your budget, current Mexican Fenders and Squires are a good place to start, and either a Precision or a Jazz bass will be fine (see descriptions below).

Strings

Since the electric bass is easier to play, changing strings is not a big issue. Generally speaking, you'll want a deep, round sound for jazz band, and you can get this sound by using flatwound strings. These strings have a stronger fundamental warm and dark sound. Most basses come with roundwound strings, and they are generally brighter. Mind you, having the strings on for a long time will reduce their brightness, and they will become warmer and darker sounding. However, keep in mind that the differences in sound and feel of the string are such that for a beginning student it can feel like a new instrument!

Pickups

The other point about electric bass is understanding the "electric" part of the instrument. On acoustic bass, the tone is mostly achieved by the player, but on electric bass, the bassist can control his or her tone by manipulating the controls on the instrument and the amplifier. Many young bass students focus primarily on playing the instrument and often do not know anything about the electronics beyond plugging the instrument into the amplifier, turning it on, and adjusting the volume. As a band director, you can help your bassists by teaching them how to dial in a good tone.

A pickup captures the sound vibrations from the string and converts them into an electric signal through an amplifier. Electric basses typically have one or two pickups, sometimes more, but not that often. Figure 2.3 is an example of a bass with a single pickup, the Fender Precision bass.

The original electric bass, to this day it is still a popular brand among bassists of all skill levels and styles. Having one pickup makes it simple since there are just two knobs: volume (the knob closer to the player) and tone. The ideal jazz bass sound is round and warm, so for this type of bass, simply turn the tone knob all the way to three-quarters of the way down so that the low-end frequencies are emphasized. If the tone is all the way up, the high-end frequencies will be emphasized and will sound trebley. Figure 2.4 is the

FIGURE 2.4
Electric bass—with two pickups

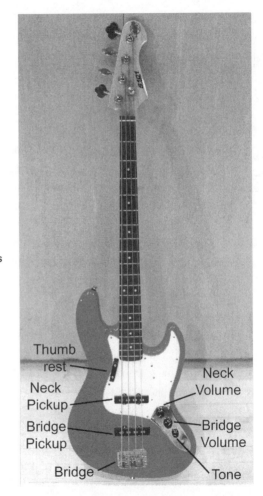

Fender Jazz Bass with a two-pickup configuration, one closer to the neck (neck pickup) and the other closer to the bridge (bridge pickup).

This bass has three knobs: the first (closer to the strings neck) controls the volume for the neck pickup, the middle controls the volume for the bridge pickup, and the third controls the tone. The bridge pickup has a brighter, nasal tone, and the neck pickup produces a warmer, rounder tone; therefore, for jazz band you'll want to have the bridge pickup volume off and the neck pickup volume on. Again, having the tone knob three-quarters of the way down will create a sound that is appropriate for jazz ensemble.

Keep in mind that these are recommended settings for jazz ensemble. If you play rock, funk, or soul arrangements, altering the tone will vary depending upon the chart. However, for swing-based charts this is a good starting point in learning how to dial a good tone for your electric bassist. The knobs on the instrument will vary depending on your bass brand, but they all relate to either volume or tone control. Some brands have up to three tone knobs with low, mid, and high, while some Jazz-style basses will have a master volume and a knob that pans between the two pickups. Determining the number of pickups on the bass will help you figure out the knobs on the bass.

Amplifiers

For electric players, dialing in a good sound on an amplifier (amp) is a skill as necessary as playing a scale. Instruments like the piano, violin, or clarinet use their own bodies to amplify themselves, so they are complete instruments. The electric bass, however, is not complete without the amplifier and needs it for volume. The amplifier is so important that having a quality amp with a cheap instrument is better than the other way around, as a quality instrument cannot make up for the deficiencies of a cheap amplifier. Finally, it is imperative that you use a bass amp and not run the bass through a keyboard or guitar amp. Those amplifiers are designed for instruments with higher frequencies, so using them runs the risk of permanently damaging those amps.

Types of Amplifiers

First off, there are several types of bass amplifiers, and the most common are *combo amps*. They consist of the amplifier (which amplifies the sound) and the speaker cabinet in one. They are also manufactured and sold separately, thus enabling you to mix and match amplifiers and cabinets, but a combo amp is the most practical.

A clean sound (meaning without any effects) is necessary for jazz band, so, volume wise, you will need a strong enough amplifier that can push enough volume to be heard and without blowing out the amp or distorting the sound. Compared to guitar amps, bass amps require more wattage for the low frequencies, so you'll need one with at least 150 watts for big band. Any lower, and you will be pushing the limits of your amp, where you run the risk of damaging your amp permanently. With three hundred watts, you have a lot of room for volume without pushing your amp's limits. If the volume dials on the amplifer are past one or two o'clock, then you are pushing your amp a lot. Most practice amps run between fifteen and thirty watts.

Also affecting the volume is the size of the speaker cone. For bass amps, the three main sizes are ten, twelve, and fifteen inches. Smaller amps also come in eight inches or smaller, but twelve- and fifteen-inch sizes are ideal for getting a nice, full sound in a large auditorium. You can still get a good sound from a ten-inch speaker, though keep in mind that you will likely be pushing the amp a lot in order to be heard. The numbers associated with the amps tend to be named after their wattage power or their speaker size. For example, an Ampeg BA115 has one hundred watts in one fifteen-inch speaker, while the Gallien-Krueger MB150 has 150 watts in a ten-inch speaker.

Understanding the Dials

Sometimes the first challenge of an amplifier is finding where the power button is! It is often located on the front on the right, but, depending on the brand, it might be on the back of the amp. To make things more confusing, some amplifiers have standby or speaker switches, which shut the speakers off while still powering the amp.

Many amplifiers come with several inputs for a quarter-inch plug, and it can be confusing to determine which one to plug into. Sometimes there will be two inputs marked 0dB and −15dB—these are for passive and active electric basses, respectively. Since active basses send a stronger signal, an input designed for these basses does not boost an already hot signal. The majority of basses are passive, and it won't really matter which you plug into.

Moving on to the dials, the most important ones for you to familiarize yourself with are volume and equalization. If there are other knobs, they aren't as important for the sound, and you needn't worry about those except to make sure that they are in the "off" position!

Many amplifiers tend to have two volume knobs: one called "gain" (sometimes called "input" or "preamp") and the other "master." Gain controls the initial stage of your instrument's signal and controls the shape of your sound. It also colors the tone, and having a lot of gain can overdrive the sound. Obviously not ideal for a jazz band, the gain should be kept in check. The master volume, which controls the power amp, controls the overall strength of the sound. While playing, the volume on the bass should be on maximum for the full tone of the instrument. Therefore, the bassist should adjust the volume on the amp to determine an ideal volume.

Equalization

For equalization (EQ), it is the same as the settings on your stereo. If that is still a mystery to you, then listen to a song on your computer with iTunes (with good headphones) and open the Equalizer window (iTunes > Window > Equalizer), at which point you will see a ten-band equalizer that controls (from left to right) the lows to the highs. Experimenting with this feature and the different settings will help you understand the basics of sound equalization. Some bass amplifiers will have this ten-band style of EQ, but mostly there are at least three knobs with some variation of bass, mid, and treble (see figure 2.5).

So what is a bass knob on a bass amplifier? Well simply, the "bass" feature on amplifiers refers to the low-end frequencies of the note. Turning the bass knob all the way down on your amplifier while turning up the mid and high

FIGURE 2.5
Sample amplifier interface

will result in a bass sound with no low end. It will be very thin and trebley, similar to the sound heard through a transistor radio.

Now comes the hard part: determining the proper EQ setting for the room. Yes, the sound from the amplifier will change depending on the size of the room, what the room is made of, and how much open space there is. This is an ongoing source of frustration for even the most seasoned musician, but learning how to recognize important factors that affect the sound (like whether there is a rug, the number of people in the room, etc.) will help you better control the EQ.

Fortunately, you will have practice in getting a good sound in your rehearsal room. Just remember that sound vastly changes as you move into your performance space, which is often larger, with more space for sound to travel in. Even more frustrating is realizing that the sound in the dress rehearsal in a big, empty space changes with people in the room during the concert, as bodies soak up sound. So, come concert time, be sure to leave ample time for a sound check and make sure to re-EQ the electric instruments to achieve a clear and even sound.

How you dial in your sound will depend on many factors, but the best place to start is to place everything at twelve o'clock (which is right in the middle) and then adjust from there. Thinking of the tone dials as having five options (off, nine o'clock, twelve o'clock, three o'clock, and maximum) will help you understand the science of adjusting the dials to get a good sound.

You will want to have a bass sound with adequate volume and a well-defined tone with a strong attack. With acoustic basses, the biggest rule is that "treble" equals trouble! So, make sure that the treble is not set too high. They also tend to have more natural low-end frequencies and are often too "boomy" in concert. This is easily remedied by bringing the bass (or low), and perhaps the mids, down to ten o'clock. This may seem counterintuitive for a bass sound, but with an instrument that already produces strong, low fundamentals, added lows from the room and the amplifier can overload or exaggerate the sound. TIP: Once you find a sound that you like, take a picture of the interface for later use.

The only other part of the amp to worry about is whether it has an XLR output. Having this feature enables you to wire the signal from the amplifier through the house sound system. This is icing on the cake but can be a huge boost when playing larger venues.

PERFORMANCE PRACTICE

Acoustic Bass Technique

For acoustic bass, basically the nut of the instrument should be at about eyebrow level so the endpin should be adjusted accordingly. The bass itself is not perpendicular to the player but held at an angle with the left leg a half-step out to hold the bass in position (see figure 2.6).

Ideally the bass should stand on its own without the player's hands. Having the bass at the proper height will enable proper arm and hand positions. The left elbow should be raised up and should be just a bit lower than the left hand. Electric bassists who sit should use a strap so as not to balance the instrument while playing. Sitting bassists, regardless of acoustic or electric, should have both feet firmly planted on the ground. This creates a center of gravity for the bassist and is essential given the role of the instrument (see figure 2.7).

FIGURE 2.6

FIGURE 2.7

For the right hand, many beginning acoustic bass players play "electric bass" technique with their fingers perpendicular to the strings (see figure 2.8).

FIGURE 2.8
Right-hand technique:
electric bass style

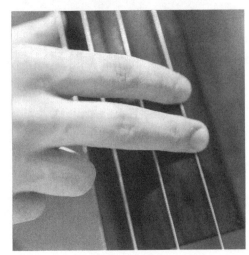

But if they pluck with their fingers parallel to the strings, or pointing downward, then they'll be able to get more flesh contact with the string, resulting in a bigger sound (see figure 2.9).

FIGURE 2.9
Right-hand technique: finger down

The right hand should remain on the lower part of the fingerboard for a more percussive attack. The key to both techniques is to have the thumb firmly anchored on the edge of the fingerboard, which minimizes excessive hand movements and promotes efficiency (see figure 2.10).

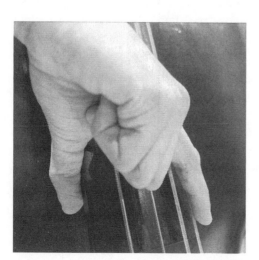

FIGURE 2.10
Anchored thumb
on the fingerboard

Digging In

A lot of emphasis on jazz bass is on the choice of notes, but that is only part of the story. Remember that everyone in the band is a drummer, therefore everyone is responsible for the groove. Bassists can emphasize this by "digging in."

In practical terms this means that the bassist plucks each note by playing with a heavier touch while using more finger on the string. By doing so, the bass line will be louder, more present, and with a defined attack or "start" to the note. Having a more defined note makes it easier to hear, and it gives something for the drummer, and the band, to play along to. As I mentioned earlier, this is a physically taxing process but makes for a stronger groove and emphasizes the rhythms. At the heart of jazz bass playing is a rhythmic function that is shared with the drums, and digging in brings out this feature. Most young bassists learn that they can simply turn up the amplifier to be louder; however, this often results in a light touch. Have your bassist play a walking bass line but have them mute their notes with their left hand, similar to figure 2.11.

FIGURE 2.11
Percussive effect of the bass line

All you'll hear is a percussive thud made by the player's finger against the string. If it is quiet, then ask your bassist to dig in or to pluck with more force. It is a small change but one that makes a huge impact on the groove.

Groove

Bassists with drummers establish the groove, and in order to do so, regardless of style, their eighth-note feels need to be matched. If the bass player feels a rock chart with a slight accent on the off beat, but the drummer feels it with an accent on the downbeat, then there is a serious contradiction of opinion, which will result in no groove. This needs to be evened out, and one or the other needs to adjust or they need to meet halfway. If the music does not feel right to you, start with the bass and drums and see whether they are together.

If your bass player is not grooving too hard or does not understand the concept, they can learn by leaning on someone else who does. I have outlined above a number of performance techniques that will help them achieve the ideal sound, but the best way to understand groove is to listen to how professional bass players groove. There is an abundance of great recordings and great bass players out there that can serve as inspiration. Have them sing back the bass lines to aurally articulate what they should be doing.

Swing music was popular dance music at one time, and while young people no longer dance to the music, it still inspires one to tap their feet. This physical reaction is the result of a good groove. The rhythm section should inspire people to want to move and dance.

Working with the Drummer and Pianist and/or Guitarist

The most important part of the groove is the interaction between the bass and drums. Beginning bassists can listen for the hi-hat to lock in the time on beats 2 and 4, but everyone should get used to listening to the ride cymbal. In swing-based jazz, this is the heart of jazz drumming and where the beat is being outlined.

Regardless of style, bassists should learn to hear the bass and drums as one sound and to continually judge how they fit together. This means learning to adjust their time feel or rhythms to match the drums (and vice versa).

With chord players, bassists should also tune their ears to what the pianist or guitarist is playing and to understand the parallel movement between the instruments. It will help them know their place in the tune and not feel so isolated in their role.

Walking Bass Lines

Like the name implies, walking bass lines should have notes that move smoothly from one to another, usually by step, as if they are literally walking. This means playing quarter notes that last their full value and holding the note until the last possible moment. Each note should also be of the same volume, and, like walking, one does not accent one step more than the other! Cutting the quarters short or inadvertently accenting certain beats creates an uneven feel that disrupts the groove.

Notewise, walking bass lines should more or less move by step with the occasional leap. The art of the walking bass line is an essential skill required of all jazz bassists. With the number of chords and possibilities, it can be an overwhelming task. In this section, I introduce patterns that you can use to create walking bass lines.

ii-V-I

ii-V-I is the backbone of jazz harmony, so it is worthwhile learning a few standard lines. Note choices are based on the parent tonic major key, in this case C major. Stepwise motion mixed with arpeggios, chromatic passing tones, and skips creates a smooth line.

Figure 2.12 features the 1-2-3-5 pattern, where the numbers refer to the scale degrees of the chord; therefore, flatted thirds for minor chords and major thirds for major chords and both the flatted third and flatted fifth for half-diminished and diminished chords.

FIGURE 2.12
Major ii-V bass line: 1-2-3-5

Figure 2.13 features an ascending line with chromatic passing tones. Note the different patterns between minor and major chords.

FIGURE 2.13
Major ii-V bass line: Ascending scalar with chromatic passing tones

Figure 2.14 features a descending line.

FIGURE 2.14
Major ii-V bass line: Descending scalar

Figure 2.15 features different permutations of the arpeggio.

FIGURE 2.15
Major ii-V bass line: Chord tones

Figure 2.16 features the 1-b7-5-1 pattern, which is most effective whenever the harmonic movement moves up by a perfect fourth. It also works best for dominant and minor seventh chords.

FIGURE 2.16
Major ii-V bass line: 1-b7-5-1

Chromaticism adds nice color to the line, and, generally speaking, roots can always be approached by half-step from above or below. Mixing and matching these options provides variety in bass lines.

A good way to practice these is to play four-bar patterns with the resolution to the I chord and then moving to the VI chord as a way to cycle back to the ii chord (see figure 2.17; see also Appendix A for a primer on ii-V-I).

FIGURE 2.17
Four-bar major ii-V-I-vi bass line

While note choices for major ii-V-I progressions can be derived from one scale, this is not the case for minor ii-Vs (see figure 2.18).

FIGURE 2.18
Note options for minor ii-V-i

Harmonic minor certainly works for the V7 and i chords, but melodic minor could also be used for the i chord. To make matters confusing, it is common to play Locrian on the iim7b5 chord, which contains the same notes as the natural minor scale of the i chord. So, all three minor scales are represented. (See Appendix A for a larger discussion on minor ii-Vs.) Figures 2.19–2.22 are the minor version of figures 2.12–2.15.

FIGURE 2.19
Minor ii-V bass line: 1-2-3-5

FIGURE 2.20
Minor ii-V bass line: Ascending scalar with chromatic passing tones

FIGURE 2.21
Minor ii-V bass line: Descending scalar

FIGURE 2.22
Minor ii-V bass line: Chord tones

Figure 2.23 features four-bar minor ii-V progressions resolving on the i
chord. Note that in minor, the turnaround chord back to the iim7b5 chord is
optional and instead of a VI chord the natural vi half-diminished chord is used.

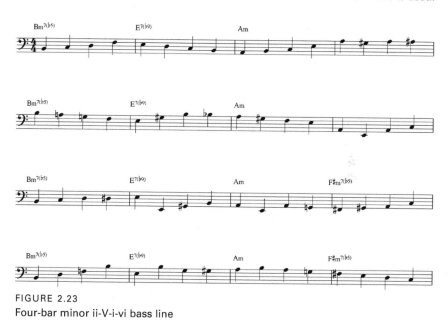

FIGURE 2.23
Four-bar minor ii-V-i-vi bass line

Blues

In addition to practicing these lines in different keys, bassists should apply
them to different songs. Figures 2.24 and 2.25 feature two different bass lines
for a Bb blues.

FIGURE 2.24
Bb blues bass line I

FIGURE 2.25
Bb blues bass line II

When the chord lasts two bars, instead of targeting the root on the downbeat of the second measure, one can play the fifth of the chord. The blues also introduces chords that last two beats; in this case, landing on the root followed by either the fifth or the third is the best place to start.

Rhythmic Variety

Walking bass lines are not limited to quarter notes. Adding eighth-note skips adds a strong sense of forward motion to the groove and should be practiced. Figure 2.26 is the same line as in figure 2.25 with added eighth notes falling on the beat with repeated notes or passing tones. Ghosted notes (notes written as an "x") are notes articulated by the right hand but muted by the left. This sound creates a thud that is percussive, similar to what is shown in figure 2.11.

FIGURE 2.26
Figure 2.25 with rhythmic skips

Writing Out Walking Bass Lines

It takes time to master those bass lines, so the best way to learn how to create a walking bass line is to write one out. Improvisation is on-the-spot composition, and writing it out beforehand slows down the process. Begin by targeting the roots on the downbeats of each measure. Then fill in the blanks with the above patterns and examples.

Improvising Walking Bass Lines

Improvising a smooth walking bass line (like improvising a solo) is tricky to maneuver. Although the rhythm almost never changes, it takes practice balancing the number of beats with the number of notes in the scale. Often bassists forget when to add chromatic passing tones and arrive on the target note early. It's particularly challenging when the chord lasts two beats, and it is no shame for the bassist to repeat notes to maintain a sense of balance.

When improvising walking bass lines, bassists should prioritize keeping time, their place in the form, and *learning to recover from their mistakes.* Eventually the "right" notes will even themselves out. Until then, learning to maintain the groove is of the utmost importance.

Walking Bass Line Summary

- Aim for roots on the downbeats of each measure.
- Aim for stepwise motion with a few leaps.
- Provide rhythmic variety including eighth-note skips.
- Dig in for a stronger rhythmic pulse.
- Match the drummer's quarter-note feel on the ride cymbal for a strong groove.

FINAL THOUGHTS

Bassists are encouraged to maintain clarity and to strive for simplicity. Like everyone else, bassists are prone to overplaying, especially on nonswing charts where there is room to add extra notes. Regardless of style, it is important to maintain a clean, uncluttered sound with minimal fills to help the groove settle in. If you listen to any James Brown recording, the bassist is focusing on the time and nothing else. There are examples of bassists grooving hard and playing a lot of notes, but that is because a solid groove has already been established. Establishing a solid groove is the bassist's number-one priority.

Finally, the last and most important thing for bassists to work on is their listening skills: gaining peripheral hearing of themselves, the other members of the rhythm section, and the soloist. This is an absolute must, as interaction and good ensemble playing stems from this trait. They also need to adapt their ears to the jazz bass sound. Many young bassists' ears have not adapted to the low frequencies of the instrument. This is particularly noticeable when they solo and are unable to hear melody at such a low pitch. A healthy diet of listening to great bands and great bassists is essential for their own education.

3

Drum Set

The drum set (or just "drums") comprises many moving parts, including percussion instruments (drums and cymbals), hardware (cymbal stands, bass drum pedal, hi-hat clutch), and accessories (sticks, brushes, mallets, etc.). In rock, drums are associated with power and loud volumes. However, they are capable of a wider range of timbres and tones that jazz drummers use to contribute to the texture, contour, and dynamic of the music.

Drums and cymbals produce two sounds: the initial attack and the resulting spread or shimmer. Electronic drum machines used in current pop and hip-hop songs often eliminate the resulting spread of drums, leaving a sound that is one-dimensional. However, jazz drummers favor the acoustic properties of their instruments and are sensitive to the resulting tones. All notes on the drums and cymbals are accompanied by an overtone that shapes the sound. Drummers with a four-piece drum set, hi-hats and two cymbals, have more than a mere seven sounds at their disposal. Instead, they vary their attacks in a number of ways that result in a myriad of sounds and tones. As a result, drums are as capable of subtlety, coloring, and restraint as they are capable of power.

Moreover, jazz drumming is about being polyrhythmic. While keeping time on the ride cymbal with the right hand, the other limbs are improvising and providing an interactive role. As a result, jazz drummers require a higher degree of limb independence than drummers of other styles.

ROLE

Drummers play various roles that vary between large and small ensemble playing. But in either situation, the primary role is to keep time and establish the groove with the bassist. Regardless of style, this is an essential function and the foundation for other skills.

In a big band, drummers work with the rest of the rhythm section, but they are also expected to drive the band with fills, setups, and cues that propel the horn lines. This is why the drummer sits in the middle of the band between the rhythm section and the horns. To many, they are, along with the lead trumpet player, the most important members of the band. With fewer musicians in small group situations, drummers have the freedom to be more interactive. The emphasis is primarily on improvisation, and they are expected to accompany the soloists with varying degrees of interaction.

In the end, different skill sets are required to play either in a combo or as part of a big band. Some players do both well, while others specialize. In both situations, the drummer must develop strong listening skills and learn to interpret the chart. The written page of a big band part is often skeletal, and the drummer is required to fill in the blanks. This is taken to an extreme in combo, when drummers are often supplied with nothing but a lead sheet with a melody and chords.

EQUIPMENT

With so many variable parts to the drum set, there are wide and often conflicting opinions about equipment. The information below is general and merely an introduction, a starting point for the drummer, and you as the band director, to explore.

Basic Parts of a Drum Set

The basic jazz drum set consists of:

- Snare drum with snare drum stand
- Bass drum with bass drum pedal
- One or two rack toms
- Floor tom
- At least two cymbals with stands
- Hi-hat stand with hi-hat cymbals and hi-hat clutch

FIGURE 3.1
Four-piece drum set (front view)

FIGURE 3.2
Four-piece drum set (rear view)

- Adjustable drum stool
- Sticks, brushes, and mallets
- A rug—one that is large enough to at least fit both the bass drum and the hi-hat so that they don't slip away during performance. The rug also protects the floors from the spurs on the various drums.

A final piece of equipment is the drum key. In addition to bringing their own sticks, drummers should have one, and, as band director, you should have your own as well. This little device allows you to tune the drums, replace drumheads, and adjust various parts of the kit.

Setting Up a Drum Set

After identifying all of the parts, the next step is to put it all together. Obviously, the rug goes down first, followed by the drum stool and the snare. For right-handed drummers, the bass drum is on the right and the hi-hat on the left. If you are unsure which side of the bass drum is which, just remember that the tom bracket on top of the bass drum should be farther away from the player. From here, place the toms on the bass drum and set the cymbal stands, with the crash on the left side of the rack toms and the ride on the right of the rack toms (see below for more on cymbal usage).

The exact placement of each piece will vary for each drummer, but they should be lined up according to the drummer's size, with the stool set so that the drummer's hips are slightly higher than the knees. He or she should not have to reach too far to play any of the pieces. It should feel comfortable and as natural as possible. Also, all drums and cymbals should be set at a height so that the tip of the drum stick easily hits the middle section. For example, if the hi-hats are too high, then the drummer will have to compensate by raising his or her right elbow. Otherwise, he or she will be hitting the cymbal with the side of the stick, and while some do this on purpose, constant contact with the sharp edge of the cymbal will result in broken sticks.

Cymbals

Pop, rock, and metal are drum driven but jazz is cymbal driven, so we begin here. The cymbal consists of three sections: the bell, which is the elevated part in the center; the body, which is the middle section of the cymbal; and the edge, which is about an inch from the actual edge of the cymbal. Hitting the cymbal in each of these parts gets a different sound. Generally speaking, for beginners, the ride and hi-hats are meant to be hit on the body of the cymbal and the crash cymbal on the edge, but there are no hard rules. Ultimately, drummers should be able to play any cymbal. The three primary types of cymbals used in jazz are the ride cymbal, the crash cymbal, and the hi-hats.

Ride Cymbal

The ride cymbal is the heart of the jazz drum sound (see figure 3.3). The time is heard on the ride cymbal and, except during a drum solo, it is the most dominant sound from the set during a performance. The ideal ride cymbal sound should be dark with a full spread. They should have solid definition where the attack is easily distinguishable from the overtones and where the resulting shimmer should neither overwhelm nor underwhelm what is being played. Since the ride cymbal is so critical to the jazz drum sound, many combo drummers don't even use a crash cymbal. Instead, they use at least two ride cymbals with one being darker than the other for a wider tonal range.

There are a few varieties of ride cymbals that drummers often use. The first is the flat ride cymbal, which is a ride cymbal without the bell. The most

FIGURE 3.3
Ride cymbal

FIGURE 3.4
Flat ride cymbal

common is twenty inches in diameter, and without the bell it is the quietest cymbal (see figure 3.4).

There is also the sizzle cymbal, a ride with small holes in the edge area that are filled in with metal rivets. When struck, the rivets rattle against the cymbal, adding another layer of sound. The cymbal in figure 3.4 also has three rivets on the bottom part of the cymbal and thus is a sizzle cymbal as well (see figure 3.5).

To get the same effect without a sizzle cymbal, many drummers can add a small chain that is draped on a standard ride cymbal (see figure 3.6).

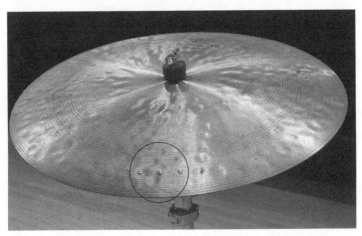

FIGURE 3.5
Sizzle cymbal

FIGURE 3.6
Ride cymbal with chain

Taping a coin on the cymbal has a similar effect, attaching it tight enough that it won't fall off but loose enough that the coin can vibrate against the cymbal.

Crash Cymbal

Crash cymbals are higher-pitched, and thus smaller, than ride cymbals (see figure 3.7). It is an accent cymbal, defined from ride cymbals by a brighter

FIGURE 3.7
Crash cymbal

sound and a shorter decay. However, this doesn't mean that one cannot "crash" on the ride cymbal or vice versa. Manufacturers also design combination crash/ride cymbals, but in the end, jazz drummers should get a proper sound no matter the cymbal. For big band, it is preferable to have at least one crash cymbal due to all of the accents in the music.

Hi-Hat Cymbals

Hi-hat cymbals always come in pairs, where the bottom cymbal is heavier than the top one (they are usually labeled *top* and *bottom*). They have their own unique stand and a pedal that the drummer uses to control the distance between the two cymbals. Figure 3.8 shows the hi-hat cymbals in "open" position, without any pressure from the foot on the pedal. Drummers often play the hi-hat like a cymbal and vary the distance between the cymbals for different effects. Videos of Max Roach playing a drum solo on the hi-hat are widely available on the internet and are recommended for those unaware of the intricacies of this piece of the drum set.

FIGURE 3.8
Hi-hat cymbals

Other Cymbals

Another cymbal used by jazz musicians is the china cymbal (see figure 3.9). Distinctive looking with the outer edge flipped upward, this cymbal has a brighter sound. Mel Lewis (of the Thad Jones/Mel Lewis Big Band, which became the current Vanguard Jazz Orchestra) favored this cymbal for its unique tone when crashing or riding. Some musicians place it on the stand upside down, so that the sharp edge of the cymbal does not make contact with the stick.

FIGURE 3.9
China cymbal

Cymbal Stand

There are at least three points of adjustment on a cymbal stand: at the bottom, allowing one to release and control the legs of the stand; in the middle, there is at least one point that allows you to control the height of the cymbal; and, finally, at the top one can adjust the angle of the cymbal (see figure 3.10).

The cymbal should not touch any of the metal parts, so there are a few protecting pieces at the top: a black nylon sleeve covers the threads where the cymbal rests, two round felt pads and a wingnut on top keep the cymbal in place. The cymbal is placed in between the two pads to protect the cymbal (see figure 3.11).

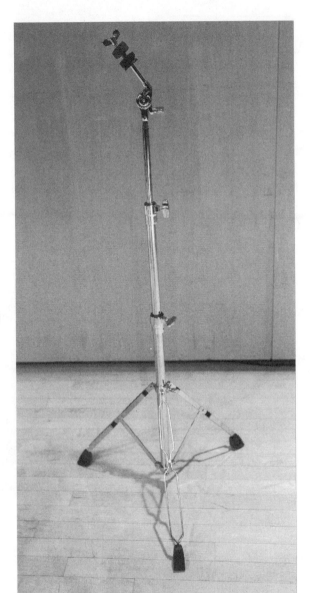

FIGURE 3.10
Cymbal stand

FIGURE 3.11
Pieces that hold the cymbal in place: (L to R) nylon sleeve,
two felt pads, wingnut, two felt pads, nylon sleeve

Hi-Hat Stand

There are two points of adjustment on the hi-hat stand: the bottom one adjusts the width of the legs and the one in the middle of the stand adjusts the height of the bottom hi-hat cymbal. Like a cymbal stand, there should be a black nylon sleeve around the pole, and a metal washer and a felt pad to protect the cymbal. There is no felt pad or screw to tighten in the bottom cymbal (see figure 3.13).

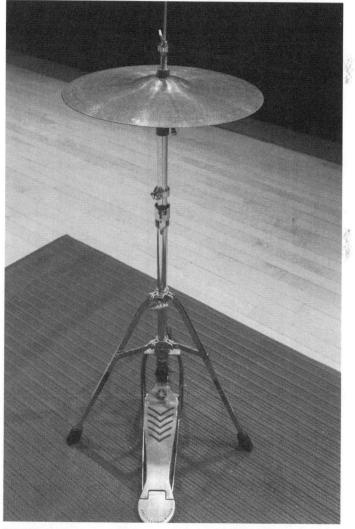

FIGURE 3.13
Hi-hat stand

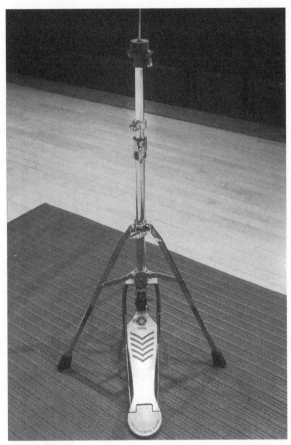

FIGURE 3.13
Hi-hat stand without cymbals and hi-hat clutch

The top cymbal is attached to the hi-hat clutch, a separate piece that at-taches onto the stem of the hi-hat stand. This piece also determines how high the top cymbal can separate from the bottom cymbal. So, if you want to ad-just the height of the hi-hat, you need to adjust both the clutch that controls the top cymbal and the middle of the stand itself, which controls the bottom cymbal (see figure 3.14).

The clutch consists of the top wingnut screw, and on the bottom there are two felt pads and a bottom screw (see figure 3.15).

To insert the top cymbal onto the clutch, unscrew the bottom nut and remove one felt pad. Place the cymbal in so that the top of the cymbal faces the wingnut,

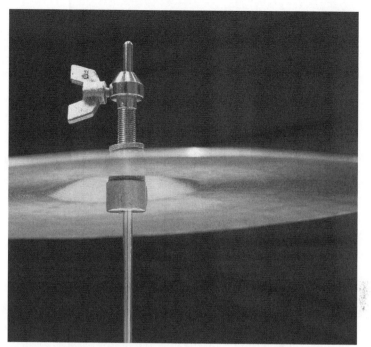

FIGURE 3.14
Top hi-hat cymbal with clutch

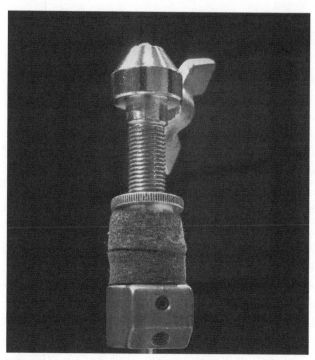

FIGURE 3.15
Hi-hat clutch

and then replace the pad and screw it tightly so that it doesn't come apart during performance. On the top side of the felt pad are two threaded metal nuts that provide tension adjustment for the top hi-hat cymbal. Adjust the tension with the lower nut so it is neither too tight nor too loose; the upper nut locks the mechanism in place. Now you can place the top cymbal onto the hi-hat stand.

To adjust the height of the top cymbal, you need to push your foot down onto the pedal. In jazz swing feel, the hi-hat is being closed on beats 2 and 4 throughout the entire performance, so the top cymbal should be high enough so that there's a nice bite to the sound, but not so high that the drummer is using a lot of energy to press down on the pedal.

Drums

The basic drums of a jazz drum set are, from the highest to the lowest pitched, the snare drum, rack tom, floor tom, and the bass drum. All drums consist of a shell, rims, tension rods, the lugs to hold the rods, and two removable drumheads, one for each side.

Snare Drum

The snare drum functions as a comping drum in jazz and, of course, for fills (see figure 3.16). Its unique sound comes from tensioned spiral wires (called snares—hence the name) that rattle against the resonant head (bottom head) when the batter head (top head) is hit (see figure 3.17).

On the side is a lever (called a *strainer*) that can loosen the snares, enabling one to replace the snare wires but also to engage a lower-pitched drum like a tom. Drummers will do this on purpose for that effect, either in soloing or in accompanying, as Vernell Fournier does on "Poinciana" from the album *Live at the Pershing* by Ahmad Jamal.

While the snare drum is most often played on the actual head, it is also common for drummers to hit the rim of the drum, called *rimshot* or *cross stick*. This is done by placing the tip of the stick near the center of the snare drum so that it dangles off the top by about an inch. While the palm of the left hand acts as a weight holding the stick in place, the fingertips control the stick, raising it up and down and allowing it to hit the rim of the drum.

The snare drum is placed on its own stand (see figure 3.18), which is marked by the rubber ends at the top where the drum is placed. Like the cymbal stand, there are three points of adjustment on the snare drum stand: one to adjust the legs, another to adjust the height of the drum, and another to adjust the angle of the drum.

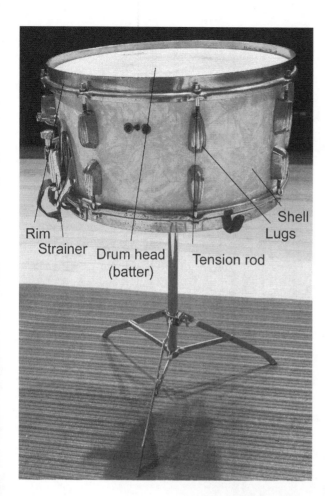

Rim

Strainer Drum head
(batter)

Tension rod

Shell
Lugs

FIGURE 3.16
Snare drum with stand

FIGURE 3.17
Snare drum (bottom view)

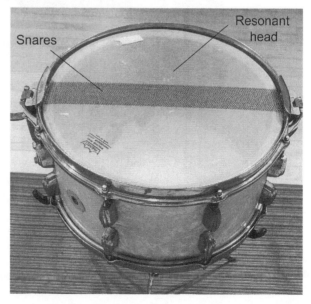

Snares

Resonant
head

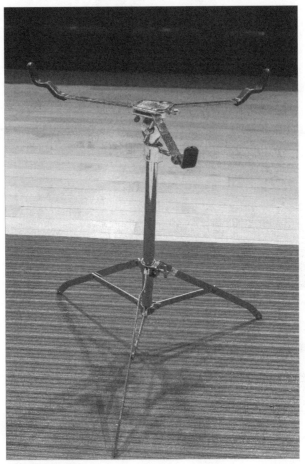

FIGURE 3.18
Snare drum stand

Bass Drum and Bass Drum Pedal

The bass drum is the lowest pitched drum; as a result, it is the quietest drum. It is held in place on the floor by spurs that either slide in and out of the drum or are attached. On top of the bass drum is a bracket where the smaller toms are mounted. The bass drum is played with a bass drum pedal that attaches to the front of the drum. While it is often used as an accent drum, older jazz styles call for the bass drum to be *feathered* (see below).

FIGURE 3.19
Bass drum and bass drum pedal

FIGURE 3.20
Bass drum pedal

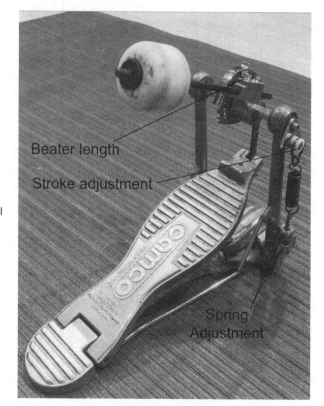

Beater length

Stroke adjustment

Spring
Adjustment

The bass drum pedal fits into the rim of the bass drum where the weight of the bass drum holds it in place. No matter the pedal, it is possible to adjust the tension of the pedal, the angle of the beater, and the height of the stem. At the bottom of the spring on the right side of the pedal are two nuts that adjust the tension. Use the bottom nut to adjust the tension, and then only adjust the top one in order to lock the mechanism in place. The tension should be loose and not tight, allowing for relaxed playing and a wider range of capabilities.

To adjust the angle of the pedal, which determines how close the beater is to the drum, unloosen the rod at the top of the spring with the drum key. Finally, with the drum key again, the height of the stem is also adjustable. If it is too short, then it will take too long to get back to the drum. Finally, there is the beater tip itself. Until the 1950s, they were made from lamb's wool, but today there are all sorts of varieties, with felt beaters being the best for jazz.

Tom Drums (Rack and Floor Toms)

Jazz drum sets include lower-pitched drums, one floor tom, and at least one rack tom. These drums are primarily used for fills but are sometimes heard in basic accompaniment. For example, the floor tom is prominent in Benny Goodman's "Sing, Sing, Sing" with Gene Krupa and Sonny Rollins's "St. Thomas" with Max Roach. The use of both toms is also prominent in certain Latin jazz styles such as Afro-Cuban, where the drum part is often mimicking an entire percussion section.

The rack tom is attached to the bass drum with a tom holder (see figures 3.21 and 3.22), which screws onto the bass drum. The holder has an adjustable arm, or clamp, that allows you to adjust the angle of the tom. This second arm goes into the tom drum itself. Having one or two rack toms is purely based on personal preference.

The floor tom (see figure 3.23) is the lowest pitched of the drums that can be hit with a stick. It is held up by three thin, removable legs for height adjustment.

FIGURE 3.21
Rack tom with tom
holder in bass drum

FIGURE 3.22
Rack tom and tom holder

FIGURE 3.23
Floor tom

Tuning the Drums

The ideal drum sound for jazz should produce a defined tone and not a thud. This result is achieved by tuning the drums properly. If you are dealing with an old drum set, you can greatly improve the sound by tuning the heads or (if they are worn out) replacing them. Of all the adjustments possible on a drum set, perhaps the most relevant and important is learning how to tune the drums. Everyone has their preferences; as band director, you should encourage your drummer to think about this aspect of their craft.

Use a drum key to adjust the tension on each rod along the rim of the drum. Tap the drum at the edge near each rod to hear the sound. They should all be the same pitch; if not, either loosen or tighten the drum to achieve the desired pitch. As a starting point, a four-piece set (snare, tom, floor tom, bass drum) should be tuned in fifths and a five-piece set (with an extra tom) in fourths. A snare drum should be bright and high pitched, as a low-pitched snare will not cut through large ensemble passages.

Drumheads

Drumheads are another expandable part of the drum that can greatly improve the sound of a drum set. They come in a range of textures and sizes, but for jazz, coated, one-ply heads on the batter side of the drum is a good place to start. For the resonant head, clear one-ply heads, especially on the toms, help reduce unwanted overtones.

They used to be made of animal hide, most recently calfskin, and coated drumheads were designed to imitate that sound. As opposed to clear drumheads, they are textured and thinner, creating a warmer sound. In rock and funk, drummers have the opposite setup with thicker heads that are tuned lower. For jazz, coated snare drumheads are a necessity. After a while, the coating will wear down with time and you will need to change heads to maintain the sound. Otherwise, brushes are useless without the textured coating.

Troubleshooting Drums

Drums are also prone to excessive ringing and overtones. Tuning the drum can make a difference, but this particular problem can be remedied by taping a piece of paper or cloth on the drum. This absorbs the vibrations, reduces unwanted sounds, and creates a more focused tone. Take a small, folded piece of paper and place it in the middle of a piece of gaffer tape about two to three inches long. What you have now is a large band aid. Place it on the edge of the batter side of the drum, and you should have an improved drum sound.

Sticks

The most common drumsticks are made of wood, and there are many varieties. They are labeled with a number (weight) and a letter (thickness), where the higher the number the lighter the stick. As you go through the alphabet, beginning with "A," the thickness begins to increase, adding weight. It is also possible to get different coatings for the sticks and stick tips, different materials (hickory lasts the longest), and, finally, the various shapes of the tip. The last variable is the size of the drummer and his or her hands. But for an average-sized teenager, 7A sticks are a good starting point for playing jazz.

FIGURE 3.24
Drum sticks

Brushes

Metal wire brushes are another must-have for jazz drummers. The wires are protected in a plastic coating and can produce a range of sounds. They are often "brushed" or "swished" on the snare drum for long tones and a smooth sound. However, one can also play them like sticks. On Miles Davis's "So What" from the album *Kind of Blue*, Jimmy Cobb plays the brush on the ride cymbal during the statement of the theme (from 0:35), but when the solos start (at 1:34) he switches to sticks. On Miles Davis's "Bye Bye Blackbird" from the

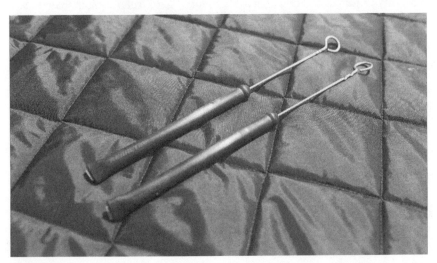

FIGURE 3.25
Brushes: closed position

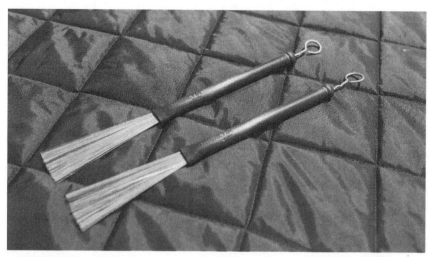

FIGURE 3.26
Brushes: open position

album *'Round About Midnight*, Philly Joe Jones plays a brush pattern on the snare during the statement of the theme.

Mallets

Lastly, a set of timpani mallets are handy to have, though they are not used as often. They are wooden sticks with soft, white felt on the end that are similar to the bass drum beater. They produce a very soft attack and are typically used for a different tonal color. Some drummers use mallets during drum solos.

FIGURE 3.27
Mallets

PERFORMANCE PRACTICE

Notation

Drum set follows its own notation. Figure 3.28 features a standardized notation. For clarity, some drum charts come with their own notational guideline.

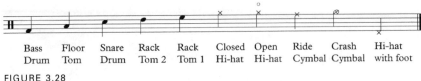

| Bass | Floor | Snare | Rack | Rack | Closed | Open | Ride | Crash | Hi-hat |
| Drum | Tom | Drum | Tom 2 | Tom 1 | Hi-hat | Hi-hat | Cymbal | Cymbal | with foot |

FIGURE 3.28
Drum set notation

Techniques

Jazz drummers must learn specialized techniques for their hands and their feet. The following outlines some basic techniques.

Ride Cymbal Techniques

For playing basic time, hitting the body of the cymbal with the tip of the stick produces a focused sound. Using the side of the stick or hitting the edge of the cymbal produces a longer, more resonant ring and is best for crashing purposes. At slow to medium tempos, the drummer can hit the cymbal for every stroke. But at faster tempos, drummers use the bounce of the stick for extra strokes. In figures 3.29 and 3.30, the accents indicate when the stick is actually being stroked. In figure 3.30, the note without an accent is articulated by the rebound.

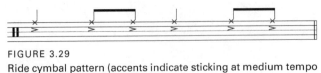

FIGURE 3.29
Ride cymbal pattern (accents indicate sticking at medium tempo or slower)

FIGURE 3.30
Ride cymbal pattern (accents indicate sticking at up tempo)

Basic Ride Pattern

Figure 3.29 shows the typical ride pattern for most jazz charts, with the hi-hat falling on beats 2 and 4. Keep in mind that this is just a template for what to do. In practice, jazz drummers vary the ride pattern, feather the bass drum on all four beats (see above), play fills, and incorporate the snare drum and the bass drum.

Since the main sound is the ride cymbal, the snare drum is played very softly and sometimes on the edge of the snare. In essence, the left hand supports the ride pattern with additional rhythms that are often independent of the ride pattern. Figure 3.31 shows a simple variation.

FIGURE 3.31
Ride cymbal and hi-hat pattern with sample snare drum accompaniment fills

On Miles Davis's solo on "So What" (from 1:45), drummer Jimmy Cobb gets a multitude of different snare tones and brings it out primarily for bigger fills that mark new sections in the form. Regarding the cymbal pattern, you'll notice that Cobb mostly plays quarter notes on the cymbal. It is more important for the drummer to establish the groove than it is to play and maintain the "correct" part.

Two Feel

Two feel in jazz means cut time. With sticks, the ride pattern is moved to the hi-hat, which is opened slightly on beats 1 and 3. Billy Higgins uses this pattern (with variations) during the theme of Dexter Gordon's "Second Balcony Jump" from the album *Go*.

Brushes

When playing time with brushes, they should be flat with the wires against the snare drum for maximum contact and a fuller sound. There are many patterns available to the drummer; here is a simple pattern to get started.

In the first pattern, the left hand is swishing the brush clockwise around the edge of the snare drum: starting on the right side on beat 1, arriving on the left on beat 2, returning to the right on beat 3, and so on (see figure 3.32).

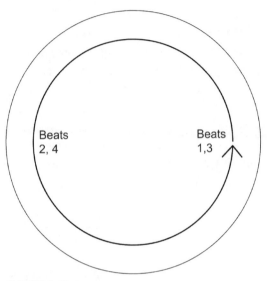

FIGURE 3.32
Brush pattern: left-hand motion

Meanwhile, the right hand plays quarter notes on the edge of the snare, bouncing back and forth between the left and the right sides of the snare. Figure 3.33 shows approximately where the brush would be hit.

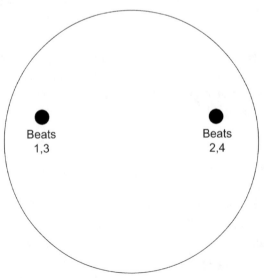

FIGURE 3.33
Brush pattern: right-hand motion

When played together, the hands are always opposite of each other so as not to get in the way. A simple variation would add the "and's" of beats 2 and 4 in the left hand, mimicking the ride cymbal pattern.

Bass Drum

It is common practice in jazz to hear the tone of the drum. On the bass drum, this is done by bouncing the beater off the drum as opposed to keeping the foot down after pressing down on the pedal, which results in muting the drum. When feathering the bass drum, it's best to keep the foot at the front of the pedal and to bounce the beater off the drum with small strokes. Digging the pedal into the drum creates tension and makes it more difficult to feather. Adjusting the bass drum pedal (see above) can facilitate feathering the drum. When playing loud accents (called "bombs"), the drummer should use bigger strokes to accent the bass drum.

Hi-Hat

Since beats 2 and 4 are being accented on the hi-hat through a jazz performance, it's important to develop good left foot technique. There are two methods: heel up or heel down. With heel up, the leg controls the motion, bouncing the foot on all four beats while coming down on the pedal for beats 2 and 4. With heel down, there is a rocking motion on the hi-hat where the heel of the foot falls on beats 1 and 3, while the toe part of the foot falls on beats 2 and 4.

Groove

Drummers with bassists establish the groove, and in order to do so, regardless of style, their eighth-note feels need to be matched. If the bass player feels a rock chart with a slight accent on the off beat, but the drummer feels it with an accent on the downbeat, then there is a serious contradiction of opinion, which will result in no groove. This needs to be evened out, and one or the other needs to adjust or they need to meet halfway. If the music does not feel right to you, start with the bass and drums and see whether they are together.

If your drummer is not grooving too hard or does not understand the concept, they can learn by leaning on someone else who does. I have outlined above a number of performance techniques that will help them achieve the ideal sound, but the best way to understand groove is to listen to how professional drummers groove. There is an abundance of great recordings and great drummers out there that can serve as inspiration. Have them sing back their part to aurally articulate what they should be doing.

Swing music was popular dance music at one time, and while young people no longer dance to the music, it still inspires one to tap their feet. This physical reaction is the result of a good groove. The rhythm section should inspire people to want to move and dance.

Working with the Bassist and Pianist and/or Guitarist

The most important part of the groove is the interaction between the bass and drums. Beginning drummers should be listening to the bassist, but they also have the advantage of watching the bassist's fingers for a visual representation of the beat.

Regardless of style, drummers should learn to hear the bass and drums as one sound and to continually judge how they fit together. This means learning to adjust their time feel or rhythms to match the bass (and vice versa).

With chord players, drummers should also tune their ears to what the pianist or guitarist is playing and to understand how their rhythms relate to their own comping. Together they can help establish a strong groove by locking in together on a short one- to two-bar pattern.

Small Group

In combo situations, drummers are expected to be aware of common jazz performance practices. They don't often get a drum part and mostly put their part together from a lead sheet. In this scenario, the drummer needs to be aware of the form, the number of measures of each section, and the time feel.

In small group playing, the drummer has a lot of freedom to interact with the soloist. Just how much interaction is appropriate depends upon many factors, including the other musicians and the style. For example, on "Strollin'" from Horace Silver's *Horace-Scope*, drummer Louis Hayes keeps his comping to a minimum, primarily limiting himself to fills to introduce a new soloist. Silver's own piano comping is busy, so Hayes was in fact staying out of the way.

By contrast, on Miles Davis's "Bye Bye Blackbird" from *'Round About Midnight*, pianist Red Garland is not as busy, and so Philly Joe Jones comps on the snare a little more. Notice the different ways in which Jones introduces new sections, sometimes playing a fill leading into the section or introducing a new idea. For example, he does both by announcing the ending of Miles Davis's solo at 3:22 with a short roll on the floor tom (the first appearance of this drum in the performance) and then moving to a different ride cymbal for John Coltrane's tenor sax solo. When Coltrane implies double time in his second chorus, Jones follows him at 4:43 with his own double-time pattern and sixteenth note fills. Later, when Garland's own solo moves from single-note lines to block chords at 6:36, Jones switches ride cymbals to match the change in texture. This is a good example of combo drumming and how involved the drummer can be as an accompanist.

Though the drum set limits the role to be rhythmic, that is not to say that the drummer cannot learn to sing the melody of the song. This gives a greater understanding to their part, as they will have a greater connection to the song than the number of measures and the time feel. Being familiar with the melody encourages a "personalized" approach. For example, a good jazz drummer will be playing Thelonious Monk's "Straight No Chaser," not just a generic medium-tempo swing feel. Drummers should learn to understand the fundamental themes and motives that mark a composition. Then they can use it as a basis for their comping and/or fills throughout the performance.

Big Band

Big band drummers should learn the various parts of the chart and when they appear: the theme, the solos, shout chorus, saxophone soli, full ensemble sections, and more. This will help them shape their part. Beginner big band parts usually have everything written out, so this is usually not an issue. However, when confronted with pages of repeated measures with a few notated rhythms, the drummer needs to learn how to interpret their part.

Fills

There are two types of fills necessary for large ensemble playing: the catch and the setup (or cue). The catch has the drummer bringing out the written rhythms at an appropriate volume. The setup, or cue, is the most important and the one that is often unwritten in the part. "Catching" rhythms can occur throughout the chart, but the setups almost always happen during louder, full-ensemble sections.

The setup is used to facilitate the entrances of the other sections of the band. Therefore, unless otherwise notated, it should match the same volume as the ensemble figure, so that the band can enter with confidence. The setup fill should also match the phrasing of the horn line. For example, if there is a short accent on beat 4 by the brass, then the drummer should emphasize this with a short accent on the snare or bass drum or both. Conversely, a long ensemble accent on beat 2 should be matched with a hit on the crash cymbal together with another drum.

There are three parts to the setup: the actual ensemble hit; the target, or setup, note that usually falls on the strong beat right before the ensemble hit; and then the fill leading up to the target note. Figure 3.34 is an example of what a drummer might actually see with an emphasis on beat 2.

FIGURE 3.34
Example of a drum chart: emphasis on beat 2

An important note is that target note that precedes the ensemble hit. It falls on either the strong beat or one beat prior to the ensemble hit. In this case, the target note falls on beat 1 and should be played with the same dynamic level as the ensemble hit that falls on beat 2. Depending on the context, a fill leading up to beat 1 may or may not be necessary. Figure 3.35 has a small gesture prior to the target note, while figure 3.36 has a one-beat fill.

FIGURE 3.35
Figure 3.34 with setup fill I

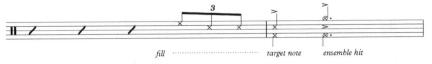

FIGURE 3.36
Figure 3.34 with setup fill II

Figure 3.37 shows another typical cue landing on the "and" of four, and figure 3.38 shows what a drummer might typically play.

FIGURE 3.37
Example of a drum chart: emphasis on the "and" of beat 4

FIGURE 3.38
Figure 3.37 with setup fill

For good examples of big band drum fills, take a listen to Count Basie's studio recording of "Corner Pocket" from *April in Paris*. Drummer Sonny Payne accents the high piano note on beat 4 with a bass drum hit at 3:54. He accents the large ensemble phrases at 4:00 to 4:03 with punches; then he plays a setup fill (4:03 to 4:06) to lead into the final chorus. He continues alternating punches with setups until 4:30. Note that just about all of his target or setup notes are accented on the crash cymbal prior to the entrance of the band.

Good setups can generate a lot of excitement, and it is easy to understand why the drummer is so important in a big band. Though the drummer is not leading the band, he or she has the power to push and inspire a band to play harder.

BUYING A DRUM SET

If you purchase a drum set, the minimum would be a four-piece (snare, tom, floor tom, bass drum with bass drum pedal) medium-size kit with wood shells, hardware (at least two cymbal stands, a hi-hat stand, and snare drum stand), and cymbals (ride, crash, and hi-hat). Wood shells, as opposed to metal, produce a warmer sound appropriate for jazz. A good starting point for measurements are (depth by diameter) 5 × 14 inch snare drum, 8 × 12 inch mounted tom, 14 × 14 inch floor tom, and a 14 × 20 inch bass drum. Larger drums can be difficult to play quietly and to generate some of the subtle sounds of the instrument. Any smaller, and the sound won't cut through as much in a big band, especially if you have any rock or funk charts.

Crash cymbals are higher pitched than ride cymbals, so they are thinner and smaller in diameter, typically between sixteen to eighteen inches, whereas ride cymbals are twenty to twenty-two inches. If you have just one ride cymbal, then a medium twenty inches should cover most situations. A good starting place for hi-hat cymbals is thirteen to fourteen inches.

The drums and hardware are generally not that expensive, but the cymbals can be. However, it is worth investing in good-quality cymbals with a dark sound. While you can upgrade the sound of poor drums by replacing the heads and tuning them, there is nothing you can do with bad or very bright cymbals. You can neither fix nor upgrade them. You might pay as much or even more for a ride and a crash cymbal than the rest of the set, but it will be well worth your while in the long run.

FINAL THOUGHTS

Whether keeping time or playing setups, drummers are encouraged to maintain clarity and to strive for simplicity. Like everyone else, drummers are prone to overplaying, especially since their parts are sparse and there is room to add extra notes. Regardless of style, it is important to maintain a clean, uncluttered sound with minimal fills to help the groove settle in. A good example can be heard on Count Basie's "Straight Ahead" from the album of the same name. Drummer Harold Jones waits for the ensemble sections to play fills and setups. Otherwise, he sticks to strict time-keeping patterns, enabling the horn lines to shine through. Drummers should maintain this level of restraint for all styles in large ensemble playing. On a complex funk chart, simple drumming can help the brass and saxophone players better sight read their lines.

Finally, the last and most important thing for drummers to work on is their listening skills: gaining peripheral hearing of themselves, the other members of the rhythm section, and the soloist. This is an absolute must, as interaction and good ensemble playing stems from this trait. They also need to adapt their ears to the jazz drum sound. It is centered around the ride cymbal but is also a combination of tones from the rest of the kit. A healthy diet of listening to great bands and great drummers is essential for their own education.

4

Piano

The piano, with its range, is capable of being the entire band and playing like one. In fact, in early jazz history, the piano did exactly that when stride pianists like James P. Johnson and Fats Waller played bass notes and chords with the left hand and melodies and additional chords with the right hand. It was a one-man band and often played solo, but even in group situations the piano maintained the same style. With the advent of bebop in the early 1940s, jazz pianists moved away from the ten-finger style of playing piano to a sparser role within the rhythm section, which is largely the style that is played today.

ROLE

The pianist's role in the rhythm section is to outline the harmonic structure of the song by "comping" chords. Comping (or comp, for short) is derived from either "accompanying" or "complementing," and it often means both. It is a very specific role where the harmonies are outlined, often in a rhythmic fashion that complements the pulse laid down by the bass and drums. It freed up the pianist to leave the timekeeping to the bass and drums and to react directly to the soloist. So, like the bass, the role of the piano is both harmonic and rhythmic.

While comping is harmonic, it also has a melodic function that the pianist can use when playing behind a soloist. Therefore, it is also helpful to think of the jazz pianist as a colorist: decorating the bass and drums with the chords and acting as a point person between the rhythm section and the soloist.

Since the pianist's chords need to line up rhythmically with the bass and drums, they need to be listening at all times to the pulse laid down by the bass and drums. They also need to adjust their peripheral listening to include the soloist. In a nutshell, the jazz pianist's role is supportive. No longer the entire band, the piano is part of the rhythm section and works together with the bass and drums as a team.

EQUIPMENT

Since jazz is an acoustic-based music, any acoustic piano is always preferred over an electric keyboard. As long as you have access to one, then equipment problems are usually not an issue. Otherwise, a keyboard with an acoustic piano sound is perfectly fine. The benefit of having an electric keyboard is the different sounds and, of course, portability. Having a Hammond B-3 sound (also called *jazz organ*) for a soul jazz tune or Fender Rhodes (*electric piano*) on a funk chart can add a touch of authenticity and make it more fun. Also, if the acoustic piano sound on your keyboard is too bright or too tinny, you can always switch to an electric keyboard sound. They are typically darker and warmer sounding and therefore more appropriate for jazz.

If you have to purchase a keyboard, then be aware that they are sold with either weighted or unweighted keys. Keyboards with unweighted keys are the cheaper option, but having a keyboard feel like a piano can make a difference for the player who would have to adjust their touch.

Some keyboards come with their own built-in speakers and are often not loud enough for playing with a group. So, it is important that the keyboard have ¼-inch outputs; otherwise, it won't be possible to amplify the keyboard. Therefore, in addition to a keyboard, you will need an instrument cable (with ¼-inch outputs on both sides; see figure 4.1) and a keyboard amplifier.

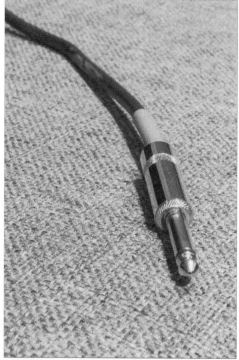

FIGURE 4.1
Instrument cable with ¼-inch output

Keyboard Amplifier

The keyboard amplifier is always a combo amp (amplifier and speaker in one) and designed to accommodate the entire frequency range of the piano. Unlike a guitar amp that is designed to color the tone of the guitar, keyboard amplifiers are designed to produce the most transparent sound without any additional tone coloring, and for acoustic jazz piano this is what you want.

Playing in a big band or combo, I recommend using or purchasing one with at least one hundred watts. The problem with a lower-wattage amp is that the sound will distort if constantly pushed at high volumes. Not only is the sound inappropriate for big band, but you also run the risk of permanently damaging the amp.

Keyboard amps are often designed with a built-in miniature mixing board capable of handling up to three to four instrument inputs. This is done to enable multiple keyboards, and since many pop keyboardist-songwriters also sing, there is an XLR input for a microphone cable. Additionally, if you need to mic your acoustic piano, some of the more powerful models (such as the Roland KC-600) include multiple microphone jacks.

Since the main control panel is the keyboard, the amp itself generally has a very simple interface with volume knobs for each of the channels, an equalizer that consists of low and high, and perhaps some extra effects. Like bass and guitar, the ideal jazz sound should be a dark and mellow one. However, achieving this through the amplifier can be a challenge. Simply begin by setting all of the dials to twelve o'clock and then adjust from there. Thinking of the tone dials as having five options (off, nine o'clock, twelve o'clock, three o'clock, and full on) will help you understand the science of adjusting the dials to get a good sound. TIP: Once you find a sound that you like, take a picture of the interface for later use.

An effect that comes with a lot of keyboard amps that can be useful is reverb. Having this option adds echo and is designed to simulate the sound of the instrument in larger spaces (such as a large hall). However, too much reverb can create a sound that is too inauthentic, but just a little bit can add some depth to the sound.

As with all amplified instruments, make sure you do a sound check prior to the concert so that no single instrument's volume obliterates the rest of the band. Volume wise, the horns should not compete with the electric instruments.

Miking the Piano

No matter the pianist or the piano, a big band with drums, amplified instruments, eight brass, and five saxophones will always be louder. Pianists often find that they cannot hear themselves during sections of the performance. Plus, in a larger concert hall, the piano often gets lost and the audience can't hear it. Therefore, you will need to mic it through an amplifier.

There is no perfect way to properly mic a piano, and there are many variables, including the performance space, the microphones, the placement of the piano relative to the other instruments, and the piano itself. The information here is general and merely an introduction, a starting point for you as the band director, to explore in miking your piano. Below is a checklist of basic items for amplifying your piano:

- Two unidirectional condenser microphones
- Two XLR cables
- Two boom stands

You could plug these into a suitable keyboard amplifier. Otherwise, if you perform in a very large performance space, it is worthwhile to invest in a mixing board and performance speakers. You can better control the tone of the piano, and it allows you to plug into a stronger speaker system. A large mixing board also allows you to mic the other instruments if necessary. If you have vocalists, you can use the mixing board to amplify the vocalists through the same system.

The piano has a wide dynamic range, and two microphones best capture the depth of sound that the piano is capable of. It's still possible to mic a piano if you only have one microphone, but then the sound quality won't be as high or it will be uneven.

Microphones are either *unidirectional* or *omnidirectional*. Unidirectional microphones are best to use for live situations, as they pick up the sound from one part of the microphone. They are easier to control and reduce the amount of feedback in performance. By contrast, an omnidirectional microphone picks up sounds from all directions, resulting in unnecessary bleed. For example, if the drums are right next to the piano, then they will be amplified as well.

Microphone cables have XLR inputs versus instrument cables that have ¼-inch ends (see figure 4.2).

If your amplifier doesn't have XLR outputs, you'll need an XLR to ¼-inch cable. A boom stand with an adjustable arm is the last critical piece and holds the microphone in place (see figure 4.3).

FIGURE 4.2
Microphone cable with XLR outputs

FIGURE 4.3
Boom stand

Grand Piano

For grand piano, use two *condenser* microphones. They are more sensitive than *dynamic* microphones, which won't be able to pick up enough frequencies. With the aid of two boom stands, place each microphone inside the lid of the piano: one pointed toward the low end and the other toward the high end (see figure 4.4).

Inside the piano, there are two string groups: the treble strings and the bass strings. Place each microphone about six to ten inches above the strings and approximately in the middle of each string group. Observe the 3:1 ratio rule when positioning the two microphones: they should be three times farther away from each other than the distance from the sound source. For example, if your microphones are eight inches above the strings, they should be twenty-four inches apart. For a brighter sound, bring the mics closer to the hammers; for a mellower sound, move them away.

FIGURE 4.4
Miking a grand piano

Upright Piano

In an upright piano, the soundboard is placed vertically against the keys, as opposed to a grand piano where it lays flat. Therefore, the sound of the piano comes from the back, and for this reason it should not be against the wall. Open the lid and place the two condenser microphones into the piano (see figure 4.5).

Another method is to point the microphones toward the soundboard. Exactly where you place the mics will vary with each piano. If you only have one microphone, then it's best to point it at the soundboard. You can also remove the lower panel (between the keys and the pedals) and point the microphone there, as this is the point where the lower and upper strings meet.

If you have no option to amplify your upright piano, then maximize the volume by removing the front boards, one facing the player and the other at the feet. You will expose the sound of the hammers striking the strings, but the overall volume will be louder.

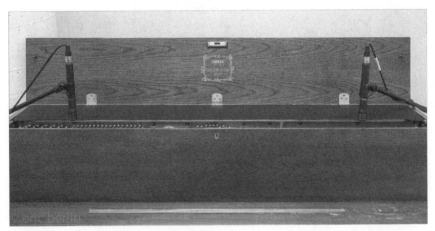

FIGURE 4.5
Miking an upright piano

PERFORMANCE PRACTICE: COMPING

The biggest challenge for jazz pianists is learning how to comp properly. The problem with defining comping is that there is no single way to comp, and how one comps depends on many factors, including the song, the style, the tempo, the soloist, and more. However, before anything else, the pianist needs to have a grasp of standard voicings and proper comping rhythms that propel the groove of the song.

Voicings

Like bassists who must learn walking bass lines, pianists must learn different *voicings* for each chord. A voicing consists of notes that spell out the harmonic and scalar implications of the written chord. Voicings typically include at least three notes and, at first, should always include the third and seventh of the chord. The root is rarely included and, instead, there are at least one or two "color" tones added to the voicing. Often, they spell out chords, albeit a different chord from the one that you are playing!

For example, unless specifically notated, the voicing for an F7 chord would not literally be root – major third – fifth – flat seventh. Instead, a typical voicing for F7 will be flat seventh – ninth – third – thirteenth! (or its inversion: third – thirteenth – flat seventy – ninth) (see figure 4.6).

FIGURE 4.6
F7 voicing

By itself the voicing no longer sounds like an F7 chord, but with the bass note, you'll hear that the voicing creates a richer-sounding chord than what is actually written. Playing voicings without the root will sound abstract at first but teaches students to listen to the bass player for the root.

How do you know which notes to add? In addition to always including the third and seventh, voicings typically include other upper structures. The root and sometimes the fifth are often not included, but this will depend on the quality of the chord (see below). The quality of the chord will also depend upon which upper structure tones are used. For F7, a dominant seventh chord without any alterations, the natural ninth and thirteenth are included. Since the chord implies the Mixolydian mode (major scale with a flat seven instead of the major seven), then those extra notes are derived from that scale: where the ninth is "G" and the thirteenth "D."

Below are introductory voicings for common chords. For now, only chords built from the third and seventh (or sixth) will be used:

Major Triad and Major 6: 3 – 5 – 6 – root or 6 – root – 3 – 5

FIGURE 4.7
Major triad or major 6 voicing

Minor Triad and Minor 6: b3 – 5 – 6 – root or 6 – root – b3 – 5

FIGURE 4.8
Minor triad or minor 6 voicing

Major 7: 3 – 5 – 7 – 9 or 7 – 9 – 3 – 5

FIGURE 4.9
Maj7 voicing

Minor 7: b3 – 5 – b7 – 9 or b7 – 9 – b3 – 5

FIGURE 4.10
Min7 voicing

Dominant 7: 3 – b3 – b7 – 9 or b7 – 9 – 3 – 13

FIGURE 4.11
Dom7 voicing

Dominant 7sus: 5 – b7– 9 – 11 or 9 – 11 – 5 – b7

FIGURE 4.12
Dom7sus voicing

Minor 7b5 (half-diminished): root – b3 – b5 – b7 or b5 – b7 – root – b3

FIGURE 4.13
Min7b5 or half-diminished voicing

Minor/major 7: b3 – 5 – 7 – 9 or 7 – 9 – b3 – 5

FIGURE 4.14
Minor/major 7 voicing

Dominant 7b9: 3 – 5 – b7 – b9 or b7 – b9 – 3 – 5

FIGURE 4.15
Dom7b9

Dominant 7#9: 3 – 5 – b7 – #9 or b7 – #9 – 3 – 5

FIGURE 4.16
Dom7#9

Altered chords refer to the altered fifth and ninth tones that are either flat or sharp. It doesn't matter which, as, either way, the altered scale is still implied. Although one can include both the flat 9 and the sharp 9 in one voicing, it can sound thick and cluttered, so stick to just one of each (see figure 4.17).

FIGURE 4.17
Dom7 altered

The fully diminished seventh chord is a symmetrical chord made up of minor thirds. So, the quality is the same no matter which note is in the bass. Therefore, rather than thinking of different inversions of the chord, it is best to think of them as a new chord. For example, the first inversion of Fdim7 is the exact same thing as Abdim7, the second inversion is Cbdim7 (or Bdim7), and the third inversion is Ebbdim7 (or Ddim7) (see figure 4.18).

FIGURE 4.18
Diminished 7 voicings

An advanced variation for the fully diminished chord is to replace the double flatted seventh with the major seventh instead. This may seem to be an odd choice, but the major seventh is part of the diminished scale and also satisfies an unwritten rule that jazz voicings should always include a major seventh interval (or a minor second). While one can play inversions of these voicings, it is much more common to substitute the major seventh on each of the above chords (see figure 4.19).

FIGURE 4.19
Diminished 7 voicings variation

A couple of basic rules for creating voicings:

- **All voicings must include the third and the seventh!**
  This is the bare minimum, and inexperienced students should start with this. The main exceptions are triads and sixths chords. Triads are a special case, but for now avoid the seventh degree for that chord.
- **Voicings for chords with the major third should NEVER include the eleventh or the fourth.**
  This blurs the quality of the chord and creates an unpleasant minor ninth interval that is generally avoided (unless specifically notated).
- **All written altered notes must be included.**
  For example, the voicing for Cm7b5, in addition to playing the flat third and flat seventh, must include the flat fifth in the voicing. The same goes for B7+5+9 where the raised fifth and ninth need to be included.

ii-V-I

ii-V-I is the backbone of jazz harmony, so it is worthwhile practicing voicings in this context as an effective way to learn voicings and to hear basic voice leading. A good way to practice these is to play four-bar patterns with the resolution to the I chord and then moving to the VI chord as a way to cycle back to the ii chord (see Appendix A for a primer on ii-V-I). The above voicings are applied in figures 4.20 and 4.21.

FIGURE 4.20
Major ii-V-I-vi voicings I

FIGURE 4.21
Major ii-V-I-vi voicings II

In figure 4.20, the Gm7 chord is built from the third while the C7 is built from the seventh. Doing so maintains the common tones and creates smooth inner voice movement—namely, the seventh of Gm7, "F," moving down to the third of C7, "E." If the C7 was voiced from the third, the voice leading would be completely lost. This is the same reason why the F major 7 chord is built from the third, as the common tones with the C7 voicing (C and E) stay in place while the outer voices move down a step. Figure 4.21 uses the exact same voicings, except the Gm7 chord is now built from the seventh.

For minor ii-V, the iim7b5 chord omits the ninth, the V7 chord includes the flatted ninth and the i chord includes the natural sixth degree. This is standard practice in jazz for a minor 6 chord, which ends up being an inversion of the vi chord, Bm7b5. Hence, both chords have the same voicing (see figures 4.22 and 4.23).

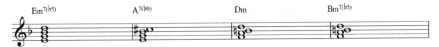

FIGURE 4.22
Minor ii-V-i-vi voicings I

FIGURE 4.23
Minor ii-V-i-vi voicings II

Blues

Figures 4.24 and 4.25 show voicings for a Bb blues. The voicing for the Eb7 is built from the seventh rather than the third to facilitate smooth voice leading. Not that it's a bad idea or wrong to move the voicing up a fourth,

FIGURE 4.24
Bb blues voicings I

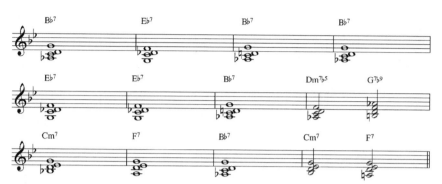

FIGURE 4.25
Bb blues voicings II

but it's important to practice smooth voice leading, and it is ultimately another tool in the pianist's toolbox.

In addition to practicing these voicings in different keys, pianists should also apply these voicings to different songs.

Two-Handed Voicings

Most jazz pianists comp with both hands for a bigger sound. Students who have a good grasp of the voicings described here should start practicing two-handed voicings. Doing so allows the pianist to get their whole body into the music and will produce stronger results.

One way to work on two-handed comping is to play the above one-handed voicings in a *drop-two* manner. Drop-two means that you take the second voice from the top and drop it an octave. Figures 4.26–4.29 feature ii-V voicings based on figures 4.20–4.23.

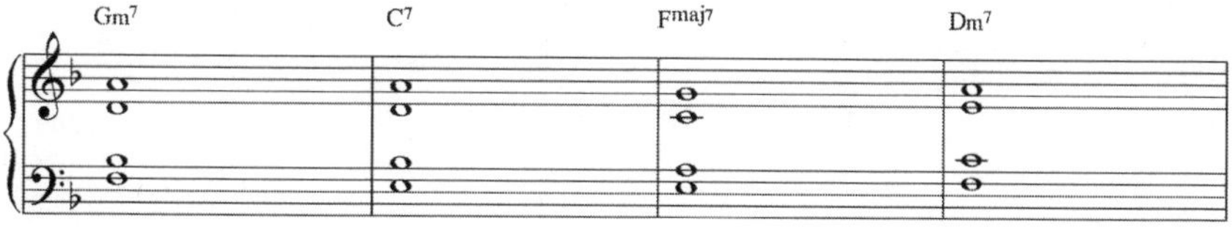

FIGURE 4.26
Drop-two major ii-V-I-vi voicings I (see figure 4.20)

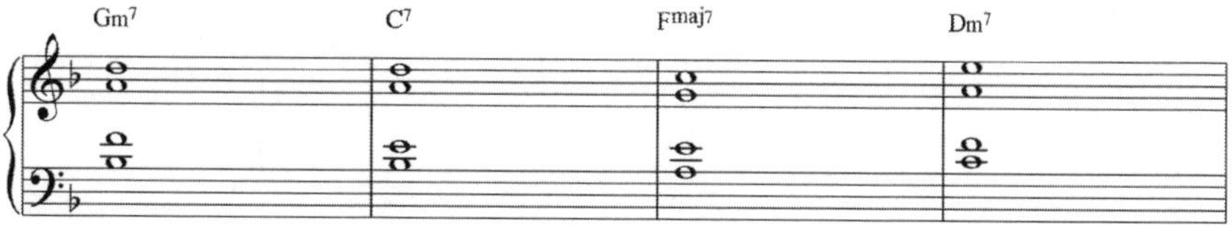

FIGURE 4.27
Drop-two major ii-V-I-vi voicings II (see figure 4.21)

FIGURE 4.28
Drop-two minor ii-V-I-vi voicings I (see figure 4.22)

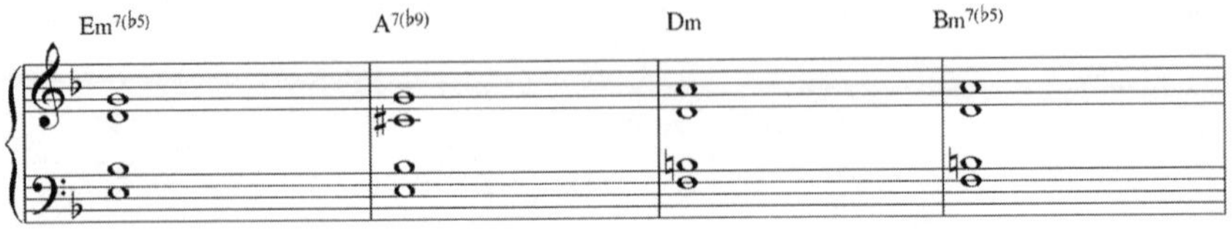

Em⁷⁽ᵇ⁵⁾   A⁷⁽ᵇ⁹⁾   Dm   Bm⁷⁽ᵇ⁵⁾

FIGURE 4.29
Drop-two minor ii-V-I-vi voicings II (see figure 4.23)

Figures 4.30 and 4.31 show drop-two Bb blues voicings based on figures
4.24 and 4.25.

FIGURE 4.30
Drop-two Bb blues voicings I (see figure 4.24)

FIGURE 4.31
Drop-two Bb blues voicings II (see figure 4.25)

Comping Rhythms

Once the "what" is more or less under control, pianists must learn "when"
to place these chords. Remember that everyone in the band is a drummer,
and everyone is responsible for the groove. Therefore, pianists should think
percussively and lock the rhythms in with the bass and drums and the first
rule is to stay away from the sustain pedal. For jazz swing feel, a good place to
start is by simply playing a one-bar pattern based on the Charleston rhythm
to get a handle of the voicings, where to place the fingers, and to feel the
groove (see figure 4.32).

FIGURE 4.32
One-bar comping pattern (Charleston rhythm)

This style of comping is often heard in shuffles where repeated patterns
are standard. Make sure beat 1 is nice and short, and this will accentuate the
swing feel.

Eventually students can move to two-bar phrases with variations on the Charleston rhythm (see figure 4.33).

FIGURE 4.33
Two-bar comping pattern

Students should feel the invisible beats to ensure a good swing feel. Finally, students should begin moving away from shorter patterns and toward a sparser approach to comping, one that leaves more room for the soloist. Playing less also forces the student to count so that they are placing their chords in the right spot. Figure 4.34 features a repeated four-bar pattern.

FIGURE 4.34
Four-bar comping pattern

Notice that the voicing on the "and" of four is based on the chord of the *next* measure. This is because the chord is being anticipated. Doing so creates forward motion, emphasizes the time feel, and augments the swing feel. When playing off beats as in the above example, it is very important that the pianist continues to "feel" the beat *after* playing on the off beat, as their chord is anticipating the harmony. Of course, they must feel the one prior in order to place it correctly, but in order for the rhythm to feel right, it must be matched with the following beat.

See-sawing between the on and off beats will help students regain their footing after playing the off-beat chord. However, after a while, students should stop thinking in patterns and instead, think in phrases. After all, good walking bass lines are rarely patterns. Bassists are freely improvising within the harmonic structure, and pianists should do the same when comping.

A good point of reference is pianist Red Garland, who emphasized the off beats with his "punctuation"-style comping. Figure 4.35 features comping on a Bb blues in his style.

FIGURE 4.35
Red Garland–style comping

In a ballad situation, everyone is exposed, so make sure your pianist has a strong foundation in building voicings. The comping need not be so rhythmic with off-beat rhythms. Instead, the pianist can emphasize the harmonies by playing more legato and sustained chords and helping maintain the time.

Bossa nova

Bossa nova comes with built-in comping patterns as played by the guitarist. If there is none, then the pianist can play these (see figures 4.36 and 4.37).

FIGURE 4.36
Bossa nova comping I

FIGURE 4.37
Bossa nova comping II

The chords should be played legato, possibly with the sustain pedal to control the rhythm. Like swing, it sounds best to anticipate the chord with a slight accent on the "and" of four. Even though they don't play on beat 1, they should still feel beat 1 as a lift off to the next chord.

If there is a guitarist to play the patterns, the pianist can play pads in the upper register (above the top line of the treble clef staff). Pads are sustained voicings that fall on the beat or are anticipated on the "and" of four, providing a nice contrast to the rhythmically prominent guitar part.

Comping While Improvising

It is important for young pianists to begin learning how to comp for themselves while improvising. However, if they don't comp, the registers become unbalanced, and with drums and bass the midrange is lost and it sounds thin. There are professionals who do this on purpose, but they balance the registers by either bringing their solo to the midrange of the piano or playing in octaves. It is a challenge for young pianists, as they are essentially playing two roles at the same time. They must restrain their solos while thinking through voicings.

Pianists learning to comp for themselves should play songs where the chords move every bar or every other bar; that way, they have time to think. It is a challenge when the chords start moving every two beats, as they do on rhythm changes. A good place to begin is to have the pianist simply play whole notes on the beat. As they get more comfortable playing the voicings, they can start playing off beats while improvising.

Other Comping Basics

The pianist should be conscious of their range and to avoid comping in the same melodic range as the soloist. A good rule of thumb is to stay toward the middle of the piano. Avoid the bottom note going lower than D below middle C, and the top note going higher than F an octave above middle C.

Volume wise, the pianist needs to be careful not to overpower the soloist. For example, one should comp differently behind a bass solo than a trumpet solo. However, no matter the volume level, the chords should be played assertively.

As a reminder, aspiring jazz pianists should learn to not rely on the sustain pedal when switching between chords. If they do, then they should be careful not to let the chords bleed into one another.

Advanced Comping

A good accompanist can also be more active in providing support. Pianist Wynton Kelly's comping behind Miles Davis's solo on "Pfrancing" from the album *Someday My Prince Will Come* is a stellar example. Kelly goes from a minimalist approach (to the point of "laying out" or "strolling" when the pianist does not comp) at the beginning of the solo (1:19) to being in the forefront of the solo at the third chorus (2:01). Yet, throughout, his comping fits perfectly within the foil of the solo and does not get in the way.

For another good example, listen to pianist Bill Evans fill in the spaces behind Miles Davis's solo on "So What" from *Kind of Blue*. In this case, Evans is interacting with Miles by filling in the spaces in his solo. This call-and-response style is still supportive, historically relevant, and exciting.

These are excellent examples of comping and a good place to start and listen. We can see from these examples that the comping instruments often have one foot with the bass and drums and the other with the soloist. The percentages are not always fifty-fifty, and they will vary widely depending upon the moment. Therefore, pianists need to develop their listening skills so that they are following the soloist while holding the harmonic fort with the bass and drums.

FINAL THOUGHTS

Pianists are encouraged to maintain clarity and to strive for simplicity. Like everyone else, pianists are prone to overplaying, especially when they comp. Regardless of style, it is important to maintain a clean, uncluttered sound with minimal chords to help the groove settle in.

The last and most important thing for pianists to work on is their listening skills: gaining peripheral hearing of themselves, the other members of the rhythm section, and the soloist. This is an absolute must for comping, as interaction and good ensemble playing stems from this trait. They also need to adapt their ears to the jazz piano sound. A healthy diet of listening to great bands and great drummers is essential for their own education.

5

Guitar

The world of jazz guitar is a different one from the other instruments. Most saxophonists and brass players have some kind of formal training: taking lessons, participating in school ensembles, and, as a result, learning how to read music. Most guitarists tend to be self-taught, progressing on the instrument by learning their favorite songs. This is facilitated not only by the wide availability of instructional videos on the internet but also by the guitar's two notational systems that are easy to learn without reading traditional music notation (see below). As a result, guitarists in middle and high school bands tend to come from a very different background and perspective of music.

There is a lot of valuable experience to be gained from playing in a pop/rock group that can be applicable to a jazz band. For starters, since most rock groups consist of rhythm section instruments, an experienced guitarist will already understand the roles of the other instruments. They may also have some ability to improvise, to interact with other musicians, and to lead a band. When rock musicians play, they are relying on their musical instinct, the "feel" of the music, and, most important, their ears and intuition to make sense of the music. All of these are important skills that jazz rhythm section players must have.

ROLE

The role of the guitar in the rhythm section is similar to the piano in that it outlines the harmonic structure of the song by "comping" chords. Comping (or comp, for short) is derived from either "accompanying" or "complementing," and it often means both. It is a very specific role where the harmonies are outlined, often in a rhythmic fashion that complements the pulse laid down by the bass and drums. Generally speaking, they provide "color" with the fundamental sound of the bass and drums. The guitar, being the primary electric instrument in most bands, is capable of providing a wealth of colors to coat the rhythm.

While it may seem counterintuitive to have two comp instruments in the same section, the guitar provides a lighter sound than the piano. It is often used as another color for texture changes, and what the guitarist actually plays will depend upon the style of the song and/or what the arranger wrote for it. Like the piano, the guitar can comp chords or play melodies and often veers back and forth between the two on the same chart. But if you're playing a Basie chart arranged by Sammy Nestico or Neal Hefti, then Freddie Green–style comping is necessary. If, however, you're playing a rock song, then the guitar has the potential to be heavily featured and to make use of effects.

Like a drum set, the role of the guitar in a jazz band is very different from its role in other popular music styles that are, for the most part, guitar driven. In jazz band, the approach is completely different, where the instrument generally does not drive the band and is primarily supportive and not in the spotlight.

EQUIPMENT

Electric guitar relies on the guitar, the pickups, and the amplifier for its sound. Additionally, there are other accessories that guitarists contend with that affect how they play, including effects, strings, and guitar picks.

Types of Guitars

For the most part, the sound of jazz guitar is electric guitar. Older styles of jazz used banjo, and different types of acoustic guitars are used in Gypsy jazz and bossa nova. But today everything is adapted to electric. There are three types of electric guitars: archtop (or hollow body), semihollow, and solid body.

FIGURE 5.1
Archtop guitar

FIGURE 5.2
Archtop guitar (side view)

Archtop, or hollow body, guitars are large, thick guitars with a pickup (see figure 5.1). The sound is a combination of the tone through the amplifier and the resonating chambers that offer an extremely warm sound with lots of bass. However, they are prone to feedback when amplified and cannot be played at loud volumes. Their unamplified volume is quite loud, though not as loud as an acoustic steel-string guitar, which is designed to project outward without the aid of amplification. Still, archtop guitars provide a warm, dark sound that is equated with the sound of jazz guitar. Charlie Christian, Barney Kessel, Kenny Burrell, Jim Hall, and Wes Montgomery all played archtop guitars.

Semihollow body guitars are hollow with a large block running down the body from the neck. While archtop guitars have a depth up to 3⅝ inches thick, semihollows are much thinner, having a depth of 1¾ inches (see figures 5.4–5.6). They represent a happy medium between archtops and solid body guitars and are the most versatile type of guitar. They are capable of producing the punchy sound of a solid guitar and the warmth of a hollow body, so they are adaptable to a number of different styles beyond jazz. Famous jazz guitarists who played semihollow body guitars include John Scofield, Larry Carlton, and Kurt Rosenwinkel, all of whom also used effects to enhance their sound.

Solid body guitars are made of a solid block of wood. Since the shape of the instrument itself isn't such a factor in the sound, these guitars tend to come in a variety of shapes and sizes. They are dependent on the amplifier for their sound and are most responsive to amplification. These types of guitars are commonly heard in all forms of popular music and are by far the most common type of guitar purchased by young guitarists. They are also smaller and lighter instruments that can be played at loud volumes and are capable of having longer sustain.

Solid body is the least common of all in jazz, especially big band, though significant exceptions include Bill Frisell, John Abercombie, and, most famously, Ed Bickert, who played a Fender Telecaster, an instrument most associated with rock, pop, and country; yet he played traditional-sounding acoustic jazz, proving that it isn't the guitar that determines the music.

Beginning guitarists typically own a guitar, usually solid body, so it is not necessary to purchase one for the band. It can be a challenge to get the sound of jazz guitar in a big band or combo for solid body guitars, but understanding the pickups and the amplifier can greatly maximize the sound of your student's instrument.

FIGURE 5.3
Semihollow guitar

FIGURE 5.4
Semihollow guitar (side view)

FIGURE 5.5
Solid body guitar

FIGURE 5.6
Solid body guitar (side view)

Pickups

Like electric basses, guitars rely on pickups for their amplified sound. Different guitar manufacturers will use different pickups to produce their own sound. Compare the pickups between the guitars in figures 5.1, 5.3, and 5.5. Most guitars have two pickups, one close to the neck (neck pickup) and another closer to the bridge (bridge pickup). There is also a pickup selector switch, allowing the player to use either pickup individually or both at the same time, as well as volume and tone knobs (see figure 5.7).

Except for the main volume, most students are unaware of what the other knobs do. It is important for you as the band director to have a basic understanding of the tone knobs and to encourage students to learn about this aspect of their instrument. Many beginner jazz guitar students will walk in with a solid body guitar that produces a thin tone, while the ideal jazz guitar sound is dark and mellow with a warm sound.

As a starting point, have the neck pickup on with the other pickups off and adjust the tone knob to about 50 percent. Never turn it completely off, as

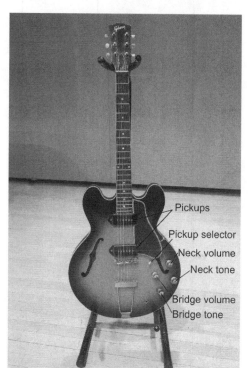

Pickups

Pickup selector

Neck volume

Neck tone

Bridge volume

Bridge tone

FIGURE 5.7
Gibson guitar

FIGURE 5.8
Fender Stratocaster

all the highs will be eliminated and the sound will be muddy. While this will not sound like an archtop guitar, it will enable a dark tone and eliminate any bright or nasal tones. Fender Stratocasters are the most popular type of guitar (see figure 5.8).

With three pickups, the pickup selector allows five possible combinations of pickups. From left to right (from the point of view of the player), the combinations are:

1. Neck pickup (tone knob 1 only)
2. Neck and middle pickup (both knobs)
3. Middle pickup (tone knob 2)
4. Middle and bridge pickup (tone knob 2)
5. Bridge pickup (tone knob 2)

Although there are three pickups, there are only two tone knobs, and for most Fender Stratocasters the one closest to the neck controls the neck pickup and the other one controls the middle pickup; the bridge pickup has no tone control. Therefore, if only the neck pickup is on, tone knob 2 won't work. For a jazz guitar tone, select one of the neck options and set the tone knobs in the middle. The guitarist should play *above* the neck pickup. Even with the neck pickup on, playing close to the bridge will result in a bright, tense tone.

Amplifiers

Amplifiers are as important to the sound of the guitar as the guitar itself. In fact, the tone of the instrument comes as much from the amplifier as it does from the guitar. The three main types of amplifiers are tube, solid state, and modeling amps. Tube amps produce a warm, dynamic tone and are favored by musicians of all styles. Powered by tubes, making them heavy, they do need to be replaced every so often and can be expensive to maintain: a set of tubes for the Fender Twin Reverb starts at $125. Tube amps with many moving parts are fragile, sensitive to changes in weather, and potentially unreliable in performance. They are also very heavy and usually have wheels added on the bottom for easier handling. However, tube amps are strongly associated with archtops as the sound of jazz guitar.

Solid state amps use transistors and circuit boards, so they are much lighter, more dependable, and hardly require any maintenance. However, the sound is not nearly as warm and dynamic as with tube amps.

Modeling amps are manufactured with a digital interface capable of reproducing different styles and classic amp sounds and are equipped with an internal wireless receiver. Since they are computer generated, they are very light. They were designed with the idea of narrowing the gap between solid state and tube. The range of sounds available could be appropriate for a big band that specializes in many different styles and would eliminate any problems related to cheap student amps and lack of knowledge of how to obtain a tone; simply turn the switch to "Jazz Guitar."

Compared to solid state and tube amps, modeling amps are lighter, inexpensive, convenient, and versatile. The downside is that the sound, being digital, is overly compressed and can sound inauthentic; however, even if you aren't computer technology savvy, they are quite easy to use. Presets are accessible at the switch of a knob or the push of a button.

Regardless of what kind of amp is being used, one of the most important considerations is to ensure that the amplifier can generate a clean, clear sound at a volume required to play with your band. Guitar amps do not require as much wattage as bass amps, but the minimum varies between tube and solid state. For example, fifteen watts for tube amps is plenty sufficient for a band, while fifty watts would be the minimum for solid state or modeling amps.

Students who come in with practice amps will not be able to get an appropriate sound for jazz groups. However, if this is all that is available, the best thing would be to bring down the volume (so as not to blow the amp) and to place the amp on a chair. Doing so will enable the sound to travel a little farther. If you are lucky enough to have access to a PA system, then you can always mic the amp and go through the house system.

Understanding the Dials

Working the tone controls on an amplifier takes practice. Each amp is different, making it all the more frustrating to understand how to get an ideal tone, plus, the sound will change from the band room to the concert hall.

Many amplifiers tend to have two volume knobs: one called "gain" (sometimes called "input" or "preamp") and the other "master." "Gain" controls the initial stage of your instrument's signal and controls the shape of your sound. It also colors the tone, and having a lot of gain can overdrive the sound. Obviously, it is not ideal for a jazz band as a clean sound is preferred, so the gain should be kept in check. The "master" volume, the power amp, controls the overall strength of the sound. As a general rule of thumb, keep both at twelve o'clock on the dial and then adjust the volume on the instrument.

While playing, the volume on the guitar should be on about 75 percent. If it is on maximum, then the highs will be emphasized and will not enable as dark a sound. Therefore, the guitarist should adjust the volume on the amp when determining an ideal volume.

Equalization

For equalization, it is the same as the settings on your stereo. If that is still a mystery to you, then listen to a song on your computer with iTunes (with good headphones) and open the "Equalizer" window (iTunes > Window > Equalizer), at which point you'll see a ten-band equalizer that controls (from left to right) the lows to the highs. Experimenting with this feature and the different settings will help you understand the basics of sound equalization.

Most guitar amplifiers will have at least three knobs with some variation of low, mid, and treble.

As a starting point, make sure the tone knobs are set at twelve o'clock. On the guitar, the tone knob should be set about in the middle with the volume at 7 to 8. If the sound is too bright, then lower the tone knob and roll off (turn down) the high on the amp. If it's still too bright, bring up the lows first, and then boost the mids to darken the sound. TIP: Once you find a sound that you like, take a picture of the interface for later use.

Effects

Depending on the level of your student, having effects can greatly enhance the performance of a tune. Especially if you're playing a rock or pop tune, some distortion can add a strong sense of authenticity. However, you have to make sure that either you or your student has sufficient knowledge of the effect to make it effective. There is no need to purchase any effects, as many guitar amps nowadays come with a series of basic effects, but your student may already have pedals to bring in. The most important rule of effects is to make sure they add to the performance and not detract.

Strings

Type and size of strings also contribute to the guitar's tone and playability. Strings come in different sizes (called *gauges*), and typically jazz guitarists use medium-to-heavy-gauge strings. Entry-level guitars tend to come with light-gauge strings more suitable for bending notes (pulling the string away to alter the pitch). The main benefit is that they are easier to press down. However, playing chunky four-to-five-note jazz voicings with awkward hand positions can cause the lighter strings to inadvertently bend and go out of tune.

Heavier-gauge strings require more strength to fret but will avoid any intonation problems and will result in a warmer and fuller-sounding tone. Light-gauge strings will result in a thin guitar tone. For beginner and intermediate-level guitarists, medium-gauge strings are a happy medium where the strings aren't too much harder to play but are stable enough to maintain the intonation while allowing the guitarist to dig in.

Like on electric bass, guitarists can choose between flatwound and roundwound strings. All strings consist of a string core surrounded by a wrap wire, which is wound either in a circular motion (roundwound) or in cubes (flatwound). This greatly affects the vibration of the string and the resulting note. Roundwounds are the most common, but, especially when they're new, they are very bright. Flatwounds tend to focus on the fundamental of the note, resulting in a warmer and darker sound and are favored by jazz guitarists.

A cheap guitar can be enhanced with new strings. Compared to bass strings, they are a cheap modification (about $10–$15) that at the very least can improve the tone and avoid inadvertent bending and any other intonation issues. Plus, these changes in equipment often make a student feel like they have improved. It can feel like they are playing a new instrument, thus hopefully enticing them to practice more. Switching to flatwound strings is a bit of a reach for those who prefer to play rock, but a heavier-gauge string is a worthwhile change that can enhance the instrument, regardless of what music is being played.

Guitar Picks

Guitar picks are used to pluck the strings. Though they are a tiny piece of equipment, they come in a variety of shapes, thicknesses, and textures that contribute to the overall sound in terms of volume, tone, and general playability. Picks come in all shapes, from triangles to shark fins. The teardrop-shaped pick is a popular pick and is in some ways an extension of one's fingernail. As a result, many guitarists feel that they have more control over their playing.

Thickness is an extremely important aspect of the guitar pick. They range from 0.40 mm (thin) to 1.2 mm (heavy), so you can well imagine the differences in tone they produce. Thick picks produce a strongly defined sound and are favored by jazz guitarists. The last element is the texture of guitar picks. Generally, they are smooth, but some players prefer a textured pick, which allows a stronger grip and better control.

A final note on guitar picks is that some jazz guitarists don't even use them! Wes Montgomery is one of the more famous examples, and he used his thumb exclusively. Others use their fingers, which is fine too. In practice, many jazz guitarists do both: soloing with a pick and comping with their fingers.

FIGURE 5.9
Different guitar picks

Troubleshooting

Unless the neck is warped to the point of unplayability, setup on guitar is not quite as critical as it is on double bass. The guitar's action, distance of the strings to the fingerboard, is controlled at the bridge with a small Allen key wrench. Generally speaking, guitars are generally set up well enough for basic performance without harming oneself.

Below is a starting point to achieve a dark sound on a solid body guitar. Results will vary widely depending on the guitar and amplifier.

- Make sure only the neck pickup is on.
- On the guitar: volume at 75 percent and tone knob on 50 percent.
- On the amplifier: high, mid, and low knobs at twelve o'clock, and the volume should be set so that the combination of the maximum volume of the guitar does not overwhelm the horn players.

- Reverb can enhance a thin sound. It can simulate the sound in a larger room, thus boosting the timbre of the guitar. Most guitar amplifiers come with an option for reverb.

GUITAR NOTATION

Many guitarists have a difficult time reading music, and there are many reasons for this. First, the music notational system is piano centric, with the middle C acting as an important link between the bass and treble clefs. The middle C on the guitar, however, is far from a central note on the instrument. It is only a minor sixth above the lowest note of the guitar, and therefore one that is not used as often. Most guitar music utilizes the upper octave, thereby requiring a more advanced knowledge of music reading (including ledger lines) than the average beginner on another instrument.

Another reason for the reading difficulty is the amount of fretboard experience required to play a single note line. Like other stringed instruments, it is possible to play the same note in different spots on the fretboard. For example, one can play "E" (the top space of the treble clef) on all six strings of the guitar! It is impossible to know how to best finger a particular passage and when to change hand positions without enough experience and fretboard knowledge.

Finally, there are two methods of guitar-specific notation that are widely used today—tablature and chord boxes—neither of which requires traditional note reading. Since they are convenient and easy to use, they tend to discourage students from traditional note reading. Even those who can read a little may have a hard time switching between playing chords and single-note lines (or vice versa), as many beginning-to-intermediate guitarists tend to specialize in one or the other.

Tablature

Tablature is a notational system that indicates to players where to place their fingers on the string. This system has been used since the Middle Ages and was designed for the guitar's ancestors like the lute and the viola da gamba. Figure 5.10 is an example of guitar tablature.

FIGURE 5.10
Guitar tablature

As you can see, instead of five lines and four spaces for the notes, there are six lines; each represents a string of the guitar, with the bottom line being the low "E" string, or the string that is closest to the player. Each of the numbers refers to a fret number. As you can see, the system is tailored to the guitar, does not require traditional note reading, and also decides for the player where to play the notes on the guitar. Compare figure 5.11, which has the same melody as in figure 5.10 but starts on a different string, thus affecting the timbre and how it is fingered.

FIGURE 5.11
Same melody as figure 5.10 but starting on a different string

Chord Boxes

In chord boxes, the vertical lines represent the strings and the horizontal ones the frets; the dots indicate where the player places their fingers. From left to right, they show the strings from the lowest to highest, and there are typically three, sometimes four, frets shown depending on the chord. The "0" above indicates open strings, the "X" indicates the string is not played, and the curved line on top indicates a barre chord (see figure 5.12).

Chord boxes do not promote music reading, but they do promote music *playing*. As a result, you may find that your guitarist knows how to fret a G7b13 but may have no idea what notes they are playing. It is important to encourage them to understand how their chords are constructed and what notes they are playing.

FIGURE 5.12
Guitar chord boxes

PERFORMANCE PRACTICE: COMPING

The biggest challenge for jazz guitarists is learning how to comp properly. The problem with defining comping is that there is no single way to comp, and how one comps depends on many factors, including the song, the style, the tempo, the soloist, and more. However, before the guitarist learns how to comp, he or she needs to have a grasp of standard voicings and proper comping rhythms that propel the groove of the song.

Voicings

For guitarists, jazz voicings represent a major step from the basic chords learned on guitar in terms of harmony and fingering. For example, most of the basic triads utilize open strings, while most basic jazz voicings do not. Jazz voicings are typically limited to four notes, and they sometimes use only two. As a prerequisite, students should be familiar with barre chords before venturing into jazz voicings. Barre chords require the player to press the strings down on the fingerboard by laying the index finger down. This requires a lot of strength and stamina to execute cleanly (see figure 5.13).

FIGURE 5.13
Example of a barre chord being played

The best ones to begin with are four-note voicings with the root on the fourth, fifth, or sixth strings. The table below demonstrates voicings for the five most common seventh chords (see figures 5.14–5.16).

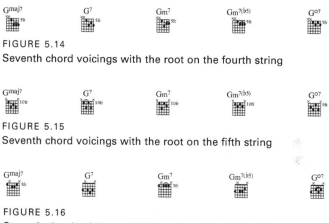

FIGURE 5.14
Seventh chord voicings with the root on the fourth string

FIGURE 5.15
Seventh chord voicings with the root on the fifth string

FIGURE 5.16
Seventh chord voicings with the root on the sixth string

Like on piano, jazz voicings for seventh chords typically include the upper extensions. Voicings for a dominant 7 chord typically include the ninth and/or the thirteenth. Therefore, even though the chart may say "Dm7," it is stylistically appropriate to add the ninth to the chord. Also, like on piano, jazz voicings typically omit other notes. For example, the G13 voicing does not include the fifth.

This is not an exhaustive list of voicings, merely a starting point for learning new ones. Eventually, guitarists will need to learn to think of voicings from the top down (from the highest note to the lowest) for a melodic approach, but this would be for more advanced students.

ii-V-I

ii-V-I is the backbone of jazz harmony, so it is worthwhile practicing voicings in this context as an effective way to hear basic voice leading. A good way to practice these is to play four-bar patterns with the resolution to the I chord and then move to the VI chord as a way to cycle back to the ii chord (see Appendix A for a primer on ii-V-I). Figures 5.17–5.20 show different ii-V-I chord voicings with the notated music.

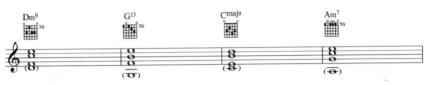

FIGURE 5.17
Major ii-V-I-vi voicings I

FIGURE 5.18
Major ii-V-I-vi voicings II

FIGURE 5.19
Minor ii-V-I-vi voicings I

FIGURE 5.20
Minor ii-V-I-vi voicings II

The bass note is in parentheses, and if you observe the other notes, they move by step. If you understand the chord boxes, you will notice that the fingerings change drastically. When the chord progression moves in the cycle of fifths (as it does here), alternating the bass note between strings almost always allows for smooth voice leading, as opposed to restricting the chords to the same four strings.

Blues

In addition to practicing these voicings in different keys, guitarists should apply these voicings to different songs. Figure 5.21 features voicings for a Bb blues.

FIGURE 5.21
Bb blues voicings

Freddie Green–Style Comping

One of the most well-known jazz guitar styles in big band is based on Count Basie's longtime guitarist Freddie Green. At its most basic, the guitar is limited to playing chords on all four downbeats of the measure along with the bassist. While this is true, in practice Green's chords often consisted of just a few notes, often limiting himself to one note per chord. Doing so creates a tenor line in the guitar that complements the bass line. He would still strum multiple strings but would mute the adjacent ones for stronger presence and rhythmic groove.

This is an advanced technique, so for most beginners the best way to begin playing Freddie Green–style comping is to limit the chords to the middle four strings of the guitar while muting the first and sixth strings. This way the guitarist is free to strum without having any open strings ring out. With a guitar pick, the guitarist should be playing short (not choked) down strokes on the beat and the occasional off beat with an up stroke with a slight accent on beats 2 and 4. The chords should be played short with the left-hand fingers controlling the duration of the chord by releasing pressure off the strings.

Piano-Style Comping

Finally, the guitar can also comp like a pianist, providing the harmonic structure as punctuating chords. When playing chords, guitarists can play with or without a pick. Keep in mind that fingers allow for even-sounding chords, as the notes will ring out at once, versus the pick, where the last notes are slightly delayed.

Remember that everyone in the band is a drummer, and everyone is responsible for the groove. Therefore, guitarists should think percussively and to lock the rhythms in with the bass and drums. For jazz swing feel, a good place to start is simply playing a one-bar pattern based on the "Charleston" rhythm to get a handle on the voicings and where to place the fingers and feel the groove (see figure 5.22).

FIGURE 5.22
One-bar comping pattern (Charleston rhythm)

This style of comping is often heard in shuffles where repeated patterns are standard. Make sure beat 1 is nice and short, and this will accentuate the swing feel.

Eventually students can move to two-bar phrases with variations on the Charleston rhythm (see figure 5.23).

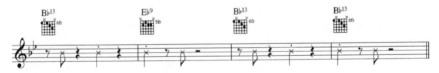

FIGURE 5.23
Two-bar comping pattern

Again here, students should feel the invisible beats to ensure a good swing feel. Finally, students should begin moving away from shorter patterns and toward a sparser approach to comping, one that leaves more room for the soloist. Playing less also forces the student to count so that they are placing their chords in the right spot. Figure 5.24 features a repeated four-bar pattern.

Notice that the voicing on the "and" of four is based on the chord of the *next* measure. This is because the chord is being anticipated. Doing so creates forward motion, emphasizes the time feel, and augments the swing feel. When playing off beats as in the above example, it is very important that the guitarist continues to "feel" the beat *after* playing on the off beat, as their

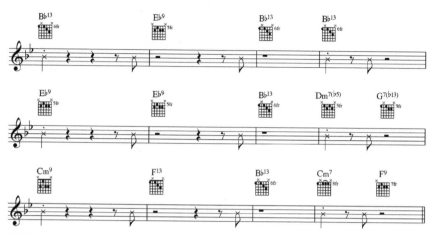

FIGURE 5.24
Four-bar comping pattern

chord is anticipating the harmony. Of course, they must feel the beat prior in order to place it correctly, but in order for the rhythm to feel right, it must be matched with the following beat.

However, after a while, guitarists should stop thinking in patterns and instead, think in phrases. After all, good walking bass lines are rarely patterns. Bassists are freely improvising within the harmonic structure, and guitarists should do the same when comping. For example, Paul Desmond's "Alone Together" on his album *Take Ten* features guitarist Jim Hall doing just that.

In a ballad situation, everyone is exposed, so make sure your guitarist has a strong foundation in building voicings. The comping need not be so rhythmic with off-beat rhythms. Instead, legato and sustained chords should be emphasized to help maintain the time.

Bossa nova

For bossa nova, the guitarist should comp with their fingers. Figure 5.25 is a common comping rhythm.

FIGURE 5.25
Bossa nova pattern I

Let the chords ring out to emphasize the dreamy feel. Like swing, it sounds best to anticipate the chord with a slight accent on the "and" of four. Even though they don't play on beat 1, they should still feel beat 1 as a lift off to the next chord. When the chord moves every two beats, the harmonic movement must adjust to the bossa rhythm (see figure 5.26).

FIGURE 5.26
Bossa nova pattern II

Bossa nova was conceived for solo guitar with voice, so it is also idiomatic to play the bass notes with the thumb. Figure 5.27 is exactly like 5.26 with the added bass note played by the thumb, while the index, middle, and ring fingers pluck out the voicing. This adds a nice coordination similar to the hands of a pianist and allows the guitarist to feel the important beats 1 and 3.

FIGURE 5.27
Bossa nova guitar pattern with bass note

Other Comping Basics

On swing-based charts, jazz guitarists should learn to comp with their fingers and to switch to a pick when playing single-note lines. This is best on a medium-to-slow tempo chart, when there is time to switch. At a fast tempo, the more aggressive sound of the pick would be more appropriate. Playing chords with fingers allows for the notes to be plucked simultaneously. Using a pick means that there will be a slight delay for the chord.

Guitarists also should not play an entire performance at the same volume. Varying the volume, particularly between comping and soloing, is essential. Guitarists should be mindful to not overpower the soloist or whoever is being featured at the time. By lowering the volume and by using their fingers, guitarists will be in a good position to be supportive.

FINAL THOUGHTS

Guitarists are encouraged to maintain clarity and to strive for simplicity. Like everyone else, guitarists are prone to overplaying, especially when they comp. Regardless of style, it is important to maintain a clean, uncluttered sound with minimal chords to help the groove settle in.

Finally, the last and most important thing for guitarists to work on is their listening skills, gaining peripheral hearing of themselves, the other members of the rhythm section, and the soloist. This is an absolute must for comping, as interaction and good ensemble playing stems from this trait. They also need to adapt their ears to the jazz guitar sound. A healthy diet of listening to great bands and great guitarists is essential for their own education.

Appendix A: ii-V-I

In major keys, "ii-V-I" is actually shorthand for iim7-V7-Imaj7. In minor, ii-V-I means iim7b5-V7b9-im. The roman numerals are derived from the home scale (see figures A.1 and A.2).

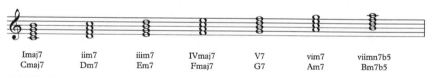

Imaj7	iim7	iiim7	IVmaj7	V7	vim7	viimn7b5
Cmaj7	Dm7	Em7	Fmaj7	G7	Am7	Bm7b5

FIGURE A.1
Seventh chords built on each scale degree of the major scale

imin/maj7	iim7b5		V7	VImaj7
Amin/maj7	Bm7b5		E7	Fmaj7

FIGURE A.2
Seventh chords built on each scale degree of the harmonic minor scale

In major keys, ii-V-I can be represented by one parent scale—in this case, tonic major. But minor ii-V is much more complicated due to the variable nature of the minor scale in jazz performance practice and the intermingling of the natural, harmonic, and melodic minor scales.

First, jazz treats the melodic minor scale differently than in classical, where the ascending scale features the natural sixth- and seventh-scale degrees. But descending, the sixth- and seventh-scale degrees are lowered (see figure A.3).

FIGURE A.3
Melodic minor scale

However, in jazz theory and practice, the melodic minor scale has the raised sixth and seventh degrees no matter the direction (see figure A.4).

FIGURE A.4
Jazz melodic minor scale

Right away, one can see how this particular scale would clash in minor ii-V chord progression. Figure A.5 features seventh chords built on each degree of the jazz melodic minor scale.

| imin/maj7 | iim7 | | | V7 | #vimin7b5 |
| Amin/maj7 | Bm7 | | | E7 | F#m7b5 |

FIGURE A.5
Seventh chords built on each scale degree of the jazz melodic minor scale

In the jazz melodic minor, the iim7b5 chord becomes a regular m7 chord. The V chord is still dominant, but if we were to add the ninth tone (in this case, F#), it would no longer be b9 but a natural 9. In order to line up with the minor 7 flat 5 and dominant 7 flat 9 harmonies, the harmonic minor scale would have to be used as well.

To complicate matters, the iim7b5 is often treated as a viim7b5 chord and thereby associated with the Locrian scale. Since the Locrian scale is the same notes as the relative minor, one is actually playing relative minor for the iim7b5 chord, harmonic minor the V7b9 chord, and melodic minor for the im chord! (See figures A.6 and A.7.)

FIGURE A.6
Seventh chords built on each scale degree of the natural minor scale

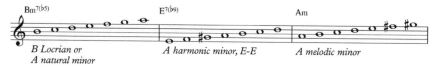

FIGURE A.7
Minor ii-V-i scales

Jazz musicians vary the minor scale depending on the musical situation. As a result, the jazz minor scale is really the natural (or jazz melodic) minor scale with variable sixth and seventh degrees: which scale degree you play depends upon the chord or the quality you wish to outline (see figure A.8).

FIGURE A.8
Jazz minor scale with variable sixth- and seventh-scale degrees

This is perhaps the single most confusing concept for beginners learning about jazz, as the "one size fits all" approach does not apply to minor ii-V.

II-V-I-VI

ii-V-I-VI is also a common chord progression and often decorated with a vi chord to cycle back to the ii chord and to maintain the two- or four-bar structure. In major, the vi chord is traditionally a m7 chord; yet musicians have the option to tonicize the iim7 chord, creating a V7/ii. However, in jazz speak, it is often referred to as VI7 (see figure A.9).

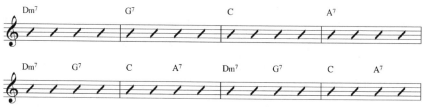

FIGURE A.9
Major ii-V-I-VI in four- and two-bar patterns

In minor, the VI chord is not used as a way to cycle back to the iim7b5 as it does in major. Rather, it is often used as a *substitute* for the ii chord. Instead, the #vim7b5 chord (based on the melodic minor scale) is used to cycle back to ii (see figure A.10).

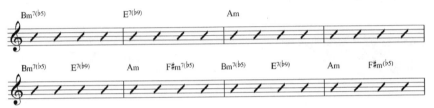

FIGURE A.10
Minor ii-V-I in four- and two-bar patterns

Figures A.11 and A.12 show the reverse of the above chord progressions, where the progression begins on the tonic. This is merely one variation of the ii-V pattern. There are also many harmonic variations (too many to go into detail here), but this example provides a starting point for learning this important harmonic progression. Figures A.9–A.12 represent the basic progression, which should be mastered before moving on.

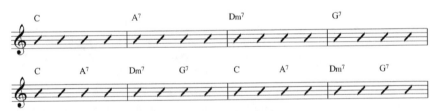

FIGURE A.11
Major I-vi-ii-V in four- and two-bar patterns

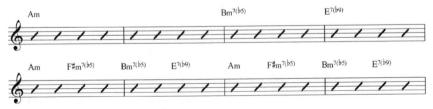

FIGURE A.12
Minor i-vi-ii-V in four- and two-bar patterns

Appendix B: Recordings

Jazz has a long history as an aural art, so it is critical to develop one's ears by listening to recordings of jazz musicians playing the music. There is an enormous amount of material to listen to, so I am only listing albums that I refer to throughout this book. This list is far from exhaustive and merely a starting point for you to explore the wonderful world of jazz.

Count Basie, *Basie Straight Ahead*
Miles Davis, *Cookin'*
Miles Davis, *Kind of Blue*
Miles Davis, *My Funny Valentine: Miles Davis in Concert*
Miles Davis, *'Round About Midnight*
Miles Davis, *Someday My Prince Will Come*
Paul Desmond, *Take Ten*
Stan Getz, *Big Band Bossa Nova*
Stan Getz/Joao Gilberto, *Getz/Gilberto*
Dexter Gordon, *Go*
Ahmad Jamal, *Live at the Pershing: But Not for Me*
Thad Jones/Mel Lewis Orchestra, *Live at the Village Vanguard*
Thad Jones/Mel Lewis Orchestra, *Monday Night*
Thad Jones/Mel Lewis Orchestra, *Presenting Thad Jones/Mel Lewis and the Jazz Orchestra*
Sonny Rollins, *Saxophone Colossus*

About the Author

Bassist, composer, and educator **Fumi Tomita** was active in the New York jazz scene for more than fifteen years and has performed with Sheila Jordan, Steve Davis, Christian Sands, Luis Perdomo, Dave Liebman, Jeff Coffin, Steve Wilson, Felipe Salles, and others. He has recorded two CDs under his name: *Untold* (a set of original compositions) and *Impromptu* (a piano trio set performing standards). His newest recording, *The Elephant Vanishes: Jazz Interpretations of the Short Stories of Haruki Murakami*, is due out in 2019.

As a researcher, Tomita has presented his work at the Jazz Education Network, BassEurope, Massachusetts Music Educators Association, and National Association for Music Education. He is currently assistant professor of jazz at the University of Massachusetts Amherst.